The Angel ...

Jean Audrey Wilson

To dear Gillian
with love and
appreciation of all
that you do

Jean

First published in the UK in 2014.

Copyright © 2012 Jean Audrey Wilson

The right of Jean Audrey Wilson is to be identified as the author of this work has been asserted in accordance with sections 77 and 78 of the Copyright Designs and Patents Act 1988.

Cover design copyright © 2014 Gary Bonn.

ISBN: 9781500984724

W hy did I want to become a nurse? Many reasons, but if I were to narrow it down to one... I confess, my main reason was that I would get back to my beloved London, the stimulation and challenges of a busy world, and away from placid, rural life.

My dear mother survived the incessant bombing of the blitz, falling "V" weapons and two forced evacuations from our previous home by the East India Docks in London. Eventually, we moved from the beleaguered city and settled down in a house un-scarred by war.

My father, a dear person, gentle and kind, had been forced into amazing bravery, again and again, during the air raids.

They had both earned the right to a more peaceful life.

But I wanted to get back to the city. With great excitement, I completed the application for the three-year training leading to the qualification of state registered nurse, SRN. I slipped the completed form into the letter box, and dearly hoped to go to University College Hospital in Gower Street.

I saw the possibility of a new, challenging and exciting life opening up. If I were to be accepted, and studied hard enough, I would also be able to go on to more specialised study.

I was delighted when I was accepted, but down-hearted to learn that I was too young, and had to wait until I reached 18.

Still wanting to move to London, regardless, I applied to the Bank of England in Threadneedle Street for a clerical post.

It was a shocking and enlightening experience. I became involved in the stocks and shares department. I hadn't thought about it much, but it was obvious, even to my young eyes, that the ethic there was the accumulation of wealth and its movement from one place to another – and nothing else. Men of all ages walked around in bowler hats, which, even to this day, I think, contained their sandwiches.

The enormous wealth of some companies made me feel nauseated, and I wasn't too enamoured of anything in the financial world. It all seemed so calculating and inhumane.

The day I received the letter from the nurse training department to say I could enter in September, three months before my birthday, I was so pleased I handed in my notice immediately.

My parents seemed to think I would know what to pack and how to get to the hospital, so I had to deal with everything myself. The only suitcase we had was of heavy leather and weighed more than the clothes I put in it. I managed to drag it to the bus stop and took a number fifteen to Aldgate. There I entered the underground and got off at Euston Square, walking and dragging the case behind me, but as happy as possible, to Gower Street and the UCH nurses' home.

Reaching the entrance, I saw a uniformed woman who introduced herself as the Head Sister Tutor. She was very kind and helped me get the case up the steps and into the nurses' lounge where there were several other girls of my age with their parents.

"Come along, Nurse Fletcher, you can leave your case here". Those were the most wonderful words I had heard for a long time. I was called "Nurse".

The relief I felt was enormous, relief at having actually found my way to the hospital. There was also my curiosity about what was to happen next, and a little apprehension – was I up to it all?

The parents gradually left, and we students got down to sorting out our room allocation. Each one of us, entering for training at this time, would be known as Set 102. Uniforms were given out and we were given a mini-schedule of where to come the following morning after we had had breakfast in the dining room.

Whenever one enters a new establishment it is imperative to learn its ways and rules. These were dealt out to us the following morning. It was made quite clear that we would be expected to work hard, study, and limit our social life to fit in with our workload.

We were taken to the lecture rooms and also the mini-ward where we would practise our practical skills at treating and looking after patients. We were also shown around the museum, situated in the basement, housing numerous different parts of human bodies—all in jars. I can see to this day half of a man's head floating in preservative. I was told the short hair on his scalp grew after his death, over one or two days.

Throughout our three months of induction training, we prepared for entry to our first year on a real ward. We became exhausted with the effort of it all. On top of this, even though we worked full-time, we were expected to attend lectures in the evenings, despite our legs and feet aching from the effort of attending patients in a long, "Nightingale" ward. Most of the patients we accommodated in a single, long room with beds either side.

We had both theoretical and a practical examinations at the end of our three months in Preliminary Training School (PTS), and were very proud when told we had reached the required standard to be allocated to wards.

We were given a white belt to show we were first-year nurses, a signal to senior staff to ensure we were only given tasks for which we had been trained.

Several things were drummed into us. Firstly, cleanliness was critically important. One had to wash hands between attending different patients, differing activities and treatments.

A second, but equally important issue was the prevention of bedsores. These can occur wherever flesh is compressed against something for too long, in this case a mattress. Blood supply can be reduced to the point that tissue dies and a raw ulcer forms. Patients' sacral areas and heels, in particular, had to be treated day and night, and patients' positions altered.

The importance of water-intake, and prevention of dehydration, were stressed from the beginning. We were taught to observe and record the patients' intake and urinary output. Our charts were regularly checked by senior nurses to see if we were fulfilling this duty.

Ward maids, employed by the hospital, were excellent. They were trained in hygiene and cleaning skills, as well as for any interaction they might have with patients.

Things such as pulleys and drips needed extra care when the area around them was being cleaned.

Great care was given anyone on a controlled diet as deviation from instructions could be deadly.

Gray's 'Anatomy and Physiology' became compulsory reading and we spent many hours finding out about the human body; it was usual to go to bed with the book to study a bit more or check on something, and waking, bleary-eyed in the morning, the book having fallen to the floor.

~

Having passed the practical and theory exams after our three-month preparation to go out on to real wards, my set faced the scary prospect of our first allocations.

We had celebrated the previous night and only one of us managed to face breakfast in the nurses' dining room.

Gathering in the lecture room to learn where we'd been allocated, our thoughts were focussed on the idea of going into a strange ward, with forty-two patients who would know we were new recruits.

The Sister Tutor stood at the lectern and gave us all a booster talk. She recognised our nervousness and the fact that we would be the most junior trainees on the wards. We were very aware of the white belts which marked us out as first-years. We would have to wear these belts for a year, only changing them when we had passed another set of exams and practical tests and gained satisfactory reports from the sisters we worked with.

The Sister Tutor reminded us to respect the doctors, Sisters and Staff nurses, any other staff involved in patient care and, of course, the patients themselves.

I knew respecting people wouldn't be a problem for me, but I felt the consultants were a little frightening and like all-knowing gods. I resolved to keep well out of their way.

My friend Stella, who was in the room next to mine in the nurses' home, was sent to a Female Medical ward. She breathed a sigh of relief, as she was suffering the effects of having broken off her relationship with her boyfriend of two years. She'd had enough of men for the moment and also wanted to avoid seeing the gruesome sights of a surgical ward. She was a lovely person, and very aware of her figure. I noticed her on several occasions give a little wiggle when she thought there was a doctor or medical student around.

It is interesting how people can be so different. To me, my body was simply the vehicle to carry my head and the thoughts within it.

The sister tutor said, "Nurse Fletcher, you are going to ward 2b, Male Surgical. They are expecting you." As she finished the list, we all headed out to our allocated places of work and training. There were so many emotions and feelings going out through that door. Fear, caution, nervousness, inadequacy, happiness and relief filled our voices as we parted.

Heart fluttering, I turned up on the men's ward. My nervousness was soon dispelled by the friendly atmosphere. In fact, during my time there, I found the patients' courage, hope and happiness uplifting.

I couldn't believe how enormous the wards looked. There were beds, beds, and more beds, two rows of twenty-one, each with a patient who, I thought, expected and relied on the staff to cure all their physical ills.

I made my way to the Sister's office and introduced myself to her. She was a shrewd middle-aged woman, who looked me up and down, assessing whether or not it would take long to knock me in to shape. Seeming fairly satisfied, she called one of the Staff nurses, a woman who dwarfed everybody and wore the red belt of seniority like an Olympic award. With a large mouth which dominated her face, she gave me a huge smile, and from that moment I felt OK and in good hands.

My first job was to make tea and serve it to all patients who were allowed drinks, avoiding those who had the notice on their beds, "No Foods or Drinks". I felt quite proud, pushing the damned thing around, until I lifted the incredibly heavy teapot to pour the first drink, only to find that just hot water came out of the spout. I had forgotten to put the tea in.

"You did well there nurse, didn't you?" The patient who had been sitting up in readiness for his cup of tea, laughed at me. "P'raps it needs to brew some more luv". With a wink and a grin he put his cup back on his locker and I disappeared in haste back to the kitchen to throw some tea into the pot.

The men realised I was new and encouraged me in whatever I did. I have to say, communication on that ward was like bush telegraph. It seemed to me that if I mismanaged something, or was a bit vague about procedure, the whole ward knew within minutes, and I was put right, though not without some teasing.

Going into the ward at 7.30a.m, the beginning of the day shift, at first I used to say, "Good morning, how are you?" I gave this up, as some patients would tell me everything, and I just didn't have time to listen to 42 symptom-by-symptom medical histories when there were bedpans rounds and blanket baths to do. I decided on a new tactic. As I went through the ward doors and made my way to the office, I slowed my walk a bit and told every patient I passed that they were looking much better, more cheerful, happier and some of the oldies, more handsome. Along with a big smile, I do believe this made people feel better and had some kind of placebo effect.

I found the male ward both interesting and educational in many ways. It was always busy and the comings and goings of patients to and from the theatre meant that we were rushed off our feet, and there was certainly no time to be bored.

Among my first duties as a nurse were ordering medicines, looking after infusions, making sure patients' mouths were clean, that they were drinking enough, or nothing – if that was what the doctor ordered.

There were several patients in for gastrectomy. This meant removal of all, or part, of the stomach. In those days this was the most effective treatment for painful ulcers that affected food intake and digestion. It was thought they developed due to stress, the example given was the stress suffered by bus drivers in the city. It was only much later that another main cause was found: bacterial infection. If only we'd know then. Antibiotics would have cured so many patients without the need for surgery.

We went through many bottles of Mist Magnesium Trisilicate and Aqua Menth Pip, which almost dominated our medicine orders for the pharmacist to make up, along with plenty of bottles of normal and half-normal saline for those on drips, plus plasma, bottles of blood and the inevitable glucose.

Some of the men were admitted with broken limbs. Often legs were placed in traction once plaster had been applied. Traction was a pulley system, which maintained the position of the bones while they healed. Graffiti is not new and the other patients took great delight in writing messages all over the plaster, some of them somewhat suspect.

When a patient was scheduled to go to theatre for surgery, they were always given an injection known as a pre-med. This was to calm a patient and dry up secretions in the mouth to avoid inhalation during surgery. Atropine and Scopolamine were the favourites used, and they didn't have any bad side effects.

Patients were not allowed food several hours before their operation, and afterwards we concentrated on rehydration until they were able to eat again. In the cases of partial or total removal of the stomach a glucose drip was set up to help with nourishment and healing.

Oral care was very important for those not eating as

bacteria proliferated in their mouths.

Several patients were admitted for thyroidectomy. This was the total or partial removal of the thyroid gland. It is a large endocrine gland with its two lobes either side of the trachea, and responsible for regulating the speed at which biological processes work.

Lack of thyroxin, produced by the gland caused cretinism in infants and myxoedema in adults. It also caused sluggishness and obesity. One doesn't see cretinism now as thyroxine can be given by mouth to counteract an under-active thyroid.

Too much of the same hormones caused a rapid heartbeat, sweating, anxiety, agitation and hyperactivity. This could often be the result of a tumour or carcinoma of the thyroid itself, and was often treated with radioactive iodine. It was for nursing one of these patients that a fellow nurse and myself were each given a strap to wear on our wrists to measure our exposure to radioactivity. UCH has always been at the forefront of research of many kinds, and as far as I know we were the first to introduce this particular treatment.

One of the things that intrigued me was that if a man has a cold or minor ailment, he is often like a bear with a sore head, but something really serious is met with stoicism and bravado, dealing with the discomfort and pain of their condition, and keeping up morale.

Humour was one way they tried to cope with things, and I found their banter gave a lift to the atmosphere. It was encouraged by the staff, who contributed too.

The theatre porters were expert at getting the right patient to the right place, and they had the kind of confidence that made patients feel secure. My own confidence grew as the weeks passed. It was good to see patients, who had been at death's door, walk out of the ward with a smile on their faces.

Mr Mulford was an example. He was rushed in from casualty and had great difficulty in breathing. He was very distressed and frightened. The inability to breathe obviously can lead very quickly to death, and therefore it was imperative to operate quickly. The doctor attending made the decision to perform a tracheotomy there and then. This involved making a hole in the trachea to bypass any obstruction. Once Mr Mulford could breathe again he felt so much better and actually began to joke with the doctor. I had to admire the courage of someone who can, at the drop of a hat, cut into a person's throat to save their life.

I met wonderful men bravely facing what life threw at them. The atmosphere in that ward was helped by the good relationship between patients and staff. The patients knew we were all doing everything we could to help them recuperate, and their appreciation was a tremendous boost to us. I can't remember any patient being antagonistic in any way, and their gratitude was obvious by their comments to other patients and to us.

The lasting memory that I have of that particular ward was of Albert Meinz, a man of about fifty-four years of age who had had an amputation due to gangrene. Subsequently his surgical wound broke down and opened up, becoming infected and leaking pus. You didn't need to be a nurse or doctor to know these were not good news.

Albert had told us he was an atheist, but one morning he beckoned me to his bedside and made certain I could hear his whisper. "Nurse, would you ask the chaplain to come up and see me? I've got to get one or two things off me chest." I told him I would, and popped into see Dr Braine, our chaplain, when I went for lunch. He promised to go up and see Albert that afternoon.

He came up to the ward later and I put screens around

Albert's bed to give them some privacy. Once the chaplain had left, I moved the screens away and asked Albert if he was OK. He beamed and said, "Although I'm not a believer, I thought I'd just like to be on the safe side". To me that was superb. Here was a man, knowing he was dying, and making sure that, if God really existed, he would be forgiven for not believing.

I said a fond farewell to the staff and patients on that ward. It had been a wonderful three months, apart from my aching feet. Several of us new nurses suffered with this. We rubbed them with surgical spirit to harden the skin, and slept with our feet raised on a pillow. This did help, and I was glad when the aches subsided every night.

~

My next ward was a female medical, and although it was interesting to go from surgical to medical, I missed the banter of the men's ward.

Very often the women there had been ill for longer and there was a tendency for some to be a bit morose when missing their children and husbands. Family ties were a bit different then, as few women went out to work and were used to being with their children all day, every day.

I learned of the many examinations needed to ascertain the state of a patient's condition so the doctors could prescribe appropriate treatments and medications. Only student nurses called "Red Belts", who were working towards their Hospital Diploma and in their fourth year, were allowed to give out medicines and these were checked by either the sister or the staff nurse.

There was little disposable equipment in those days, and one of my jobs was to clean and re-sterilise syringes before they could be used again.

To help clear the upper respiratory tract and help a patient's breathing, I would prepare an inhaler. This meant pouring hot water over tincture of benzoin, in a specially shaped container and placing a towel over the patient's head so she could breathe the vapour.

On my second week in the ward, I came across my first patient with a colostomy. She had had an operation to bring part of her intestine to the surface of her abdominal wall to overcome a blockage caused by a growth. A drainage tube was connected between her "Stoma" and a container by the side of the bed. When the swelling and inflammation from surgery settled, she was given a colostomy bag which fitted over the stoma and collected faecal matter from her body. After surgery she also had a urinary catheter, which ran into another container. As if that wasn't enough for her, she had a glucose drip, to give her sufficient nourishment while her digestive system had time to recover from the operation. This particular patient, in bed 20, only looked about twenty-five. I felt sorry for her. She was unusually young to have a colostomy; something that would change her body-image forever and may affect relationships.

She looked terribly thin and her skin was dry and jaundiced. I assisted Staff nurse Massey when the bed needed changing.

Massey said, "You must be careful of her colostomy drainage; record the amount of urine and check the intake-output chart and make certain it's up to date. By the way, Nurse Fletcher, you must give her mouth a clean and put some fresh water by the bed for her to sip". Staff nurse Massey was an easy-going individual. She knew her stuff and was very good at explaining everything to me.

I fetched the pressure-sore treatment equipment and some fresh bed clothes, swabs and disinfectant.

Changing the bed was fairly complicated considering the

various bits of tubing and dressings. We put on masks to limit any cross-infection and also to avoid some of the smell given by the colostomy drainage. Massey made a point of telling the patient what we were going to do and we tackled the colostomy drainage first.

We clamped the tubing, put a spigot in the catheter and very carefully rolled the patient on her side. By doing this we were able to treat her pressure areas, roll up the lower sheet lengthwise as far as we could, unfold and place the fresh sheet half-way across the mattress and roll the patient back again.

We measured fluid outputs, removed the spigot, un-clamped the colostomy tubing and made certain the intravenous infusion was still working. It took both of us to shift her further up the bed so that she could see the other patients, although it didn't take long for her to fall asleep again, once I had cleaned her mouth and given her some sips of water. She looked so small and vulnerable, but at least she was clean and comfortable.

I wheeled the trolley back to the sluice, where all the rubber under-sheets were kept, hanging over a large rod. Every rubber sheet we removed from a vacated bed had to be thoroughly cleaned and dried before being used again for the next patient. It was here that the metal bedpans were kept too, stacked up ready for the nurses to take to patients when the next bedpan round was due. The bedpan washer was a wonderful improvement on cleaning bedpans by hand.

Even when working in the sluice, we always had to appear clean and tidy. It was very rare to see a nurse in a messy apron, or with hair hanging below her shoulders. The ward Sisters were quick to admonish and lecture any nurse not scrupulous with her appearance.

As I gained confidence, and the patients began to get to know me a little, I felt that I had chosen the right profession and the right hospital for my training.

I made a point of learning all the patients' names as soon as possible, although it was easier, between staff, to refer to them by bed number.

It was very important to use a patient's formal name at first, as some of the older women objected to a young nurse using their Christian name. They felt it showed disrespect and sometimes seemed uncomfortable about having to rely on somebody else younger and perhaps less mature than themselves.

Several women had circulation problems, varicose veins, oedema, arteriosclerosis, or conditions relating to the digestive system. Also, there were some patients with gynaecological problems, but the severe cases were placed in the gynaecological ward where there was specialised nursing.

One woman of about twenty-five years of age, who was placed in a side ward, had lupus vulgaris which was particularly upsetting to see, mainly because it was extremely painful for her and no cure was available. It occurred on her face and upper body as hideous, disfiguring sores that would have been upsetting for other patients to see.

On this ward many tests were carried out, and we had to be absolutely certain the correct pre-test conditions were in place. Procedures such as restriction of certain foods, fluids, or digestive tests, enemas, or douches, had to be followed before medics came to take swabs, blood tests and check for palpitations. In those days the doctors used more hands-on diagnostics, going on what they heard, saw, felt and smelled.

There was so much to learn here and we students had entered a world of leukaemia, cancer, multiple sclerosis, severe rheumatic disease and many other conditions.

I started taking temperatures and blood pressures, and

recording these on the chart at the bottom of the beds. The sisters on the ward were extremely helpful and explained clearly anything I had to do.

Many of the patients had drips of some kind or other. Some had half-normal or normal saline, some had blood transfusions. This meant there were a number of non-ambulant women in the ward and they needed extra care to prevent bedsores occurring. It would have been deemed to be poor-quality nursing if they had developed.

As much as anything else, I learned that good organisation and discipline led to optimum patient care. Everybody knew what had to be done and the ward sister made certain everyone performed to a high standard. It is the type of knowledge that can only be taught in the practical situation. Words may describe what is required, but can be misinterpreted, or not fully understood. Once you have seen a process it is much easier to get it right.

~

There was considerable excitement at this time, and we were all caught up in it. So many medical advances were made during the nineteen-fifties, especially the use of antibiotics.

New research facilities opened; UCH and most London hospitals were in the forefront of research on many illnesses and conditions which, up until that point, had been a great problem in society.

Cortisone was developed and found to be a great aid to those patients with arthritis and, added to this, was the enormous life changing Salk-vaccine which had the profound effect of ridding this country of the dreaded poliomyelitis. All children were vaccinated, and it was a wonderful relief not to see a child inside an iron lung – a machine which helped a child to breathe, forcing its lungs to expand and contract, so taking in air. These machines must have seemed enormous and frightening to children, who were forced to lay with just their head protruding. Visiting mums and dads were unable to cuddle their children and give physical comfort.

Iron lungs did save some lives at a time when many died unnecessarily, but seeing children unable to run or jump, in fact do anything except try to breathe was something I don't want to experience again.

We were involved in many of these new advances and it became a never-ending learning situation that gave us all new hope for the elimination of so many terrible conditions.

One thing that struck me at the time was the discovery of the importance of oxytocin in mother-and-child bonding. As usual, nature had been crafty and it was after childbirth that oxytocin flooded the mother's system to create a feeling of love.

~

These two ward placements, surgical and medical, involved me in many less pleasant aspects of life. I had to come to terms with death.

Unless I coped with that, the frequent tragedies I witnessed would have become too difficult to endure. I would also fail to help relatives in their grieving.

Our chaplain was an ideal person for his work. His chapel of rest in the basement of the hospital was always full of flowers; grieving relatives were always welcome to sit there, or to have some counselling. Sometimes, when I felt I had had enough for the day, I used to go there and sit just for a few minutes to appreciate the flowers. I found the sense of stillness and tranquillity he'd created restful and therapeutic.

~

One day, my nurse tutor said, "Nurse Fletcher, you're being placed on the Women's Geriatric ward in St Pancras Hospital. You'll have six weeks there, and then return to UCH. You're to have a further six weeks on the Men's Geriatric ward, which has just opened."

UCH was the first hospital to develop specialised geriatric wards. Until they were ready, the patients were housed in a spare ward in St Pancras Hospital.

The ward at St Pancras was an eye-opener. Some practices wouldn't be supported today. It was a typical long ward, and women lay, or sat in bed, watching nothing very much.

Some were able to get out of bed and wander around, like old Mrs Higgs, who tried very hard to maintain her independence and hobbled around, clutching the end of every bed as she made her way to the bathroom, right at the other end of the ward.

Each time she moved from bed to bed she said the same thing to each occupant. "I'm just getting my breath back dear". However, these repeated words led to different responses, some friendly, others less so, some hostile. They ranged from, "Take you time, doll, I ain't going anywhere", to, "Don't muck up my bed will you, Mrs Higgs? I might have some visitors today", or the more extreme, "Get away and don't disturb me".

As I walked through the ward I made a mental note of any patient who had any special difficulty. A particular patient was one of these. Her bed-sides were up, trapping her as in a cage, and bandages tied her wrists to the bars, leaving her unable to move around the bed, or even scratch or blow her nose, if she wanted to.

Feeling rather disturbed by this, I asked a Staff nurse why

the patient's hands were tied

She replied, "She keeps pulling off all her clothes and it upsets the other patients. It's not nice if there are any visitors here."

The Sister was one of those who had worked in old-style homes which had used such methods as standard. I have to admit that I found it extremely upsetting that anybody should be treated in such a way. I found out later that the patient had held an important position during the war and had put herself at risk again and again for her country.

It hardly seemed right that she, or indeed anybody else, should be treated like that. I had an odd feeling that she may have been divesting herself of her clothes in the same way that Lady Macbeth continuously washed her hands to get rid of troublesome memories.

I suggested that we place her bed at the end of the ward so that just one screen could be placed around her instead of tying her hands, but nothing happened.

I was glad when she was transferred to the main hospital, and into better care, as soon as the Female ward opened. In UCH more specialised nursing care for the elderly was being considered more seriously than before.

We were always ordering more waterproof rubber sheets as bladder control was difficult for those women who had had many children and whose muscles were weakened as a result.

It wasn't unusual for some women to have a prolapsed uterus, which caused them great difficulty and discomfort until they were able to have surgery or physical support. I remember, when I was working in casualty years later, one woman who hobbled in, hardly able to walk. I found that, under her clothes, her uterus was hanging between her legs.

Another problem for some patients in the female geriatric ward was that of poor hearing. It often meant that they had no idea what was being said to them. Good nursing required a great deal of patience and understanding to repeat things carefully and slowly so that the hard of hearing could understand. A silent world is one that quickly has an effect on a sufferer. They tend to shut themselves off, the effort of communication being too great.

Loss of co-ordination often troubled these patients. I have a feeling that some of this was due to the onset of Parkinson's disease. One sufferer, Mrs B, had several falls in the ward. To give her some stability we tried to get her to use a walking stick. "I can't do with having a wooden prop, nurse." was her response. She hated the idea of any kind of aid which highlighted her age and infirmity. When we offered to push her to the bathroom in a wheelchair, we were wasting our time, until she fell one morning and severely bruised her arm. It was only then she conceded to the idea of "having a lift" if she needed to get around.

Strokes were a major cause of death in that ward. One of the patients, who was desperately trying to get her speech back, told me she'd had pins and needles in her left arm for two months before her stroke. "I didn't take any notice of it, nurse, but I did have a bad headache from time to time. I just collapsed one day and couldn't do anything. I couldn't call my daughter, and was stuck there all night on the floor, in the cold."

She was fortunate to get her voice back, because several of the patients were left with no language, poor hearing and little, if any, body control. They were reduced to what seemed to be nothing more than a shell and needed total care. More recently it's been discovered that stroke victims' brains can remain quite active, and our patients could well have had many thoughts which couldn't be expressed.

Because of the frailty of many of the patients, the bedpan round took some time. Old bones protested at being lifted onto a metal bedpan that could cause great discomfort. Very often incontinence pads were necessary and had to be changed regularly to prevent bedsores. These pads were a constant problem as lying on a damp or wet pad soon made skin soft and liable to break down, especially skin that was thin and not protected by layers of fatty tissue. We used to be very careful, and usually managed to change incontinence pads without too much discomfort to the patient.

Once an elderly patient had been admitted to the Geriatric ward, they were unlikely to return home. The Almoner (rather like a social worker) assessed accommodation and support. If both were adequate the patient was discharged. With the beginnings of home care services, like the Queen's Institute of District Nursing, which I later joined, and one or two other organisations linked to the Salvation Army or the Church, more patients could return home. It was also becoming possible for patients who needed regular injections, or changes of dressings, to stay at home with their families.

Some patients on the ward were very emaciated and clearly had not been getting enough to eat. They either couldn't afford to eat well, were unable to deal with the effort of cooking, or not able to shop. There was no pre-packed food, no supermarkets and certainly no microwaves for quick cooking. Many of the elderly used to go to the nearest butcher's shop and ask for a bone. The bone would be the basis of a kind of stew into which anything edible would be boiled.

After six weeks in the Women's Geriatric ward in St Pancras Hospital, I was ready to go back to UCH to gain further experience, in the Men's ward. The ward had been refurbished and was fresh and light.

It seemed to me at the time, that the ageing process was generally more difficult for men. Those who had managed to live to an old age appeared to feel at a loss, not knowing what to do with themselves after retirement.

Kidney and prostate conditions often caused the patients considerable difficulties, and their reaction to our care was often surly. Several had urinary catheters which reduced their ability to move around the ward and meet the other patients, although getting up and sitting at a central table was encouraged for those who could manage to get there.

Physiotherapy was not well developed then, coming later when it was realised that movement, however limited, was valuable in maintaining flexibility. Physiotherapy grew from the work of several doctors who endeavoured to vastly improve facilities for older people.

Those patients beginning to suffer from dementia, were no longer placed in asylums (later referred to as mental hospitals) although, if the disease worsened too much, that remained the only course of action available.

Many men at that time had been involved in the sport of boxing. In the East End, that and dog racing were the most popular spectator sports.

With so many men boxing, it was inevitable that some would suffer the results of repeated blows to the head. Ringing in the ears, or tinnitus, was devastating to two men in particular. "It's always there nurse, during the day, during the night, I can't get away from it. It's driving me mad." There was no cure, and one doctor thought that Fred, a veteran of the First World War, had probably experienced shells bursting near him during his time in the trenches. These days it is possible to cancel out tinnitus by using sonic devices.

One patient, a Mr S, suffered from ongoing eye disease. This was thought to have been caused by his work in the docks where the men loading and off-loading the cargoes picked up diseases carried by rats on the ships. Nothing seemed to work for Mr S and it was only the use of penicillin which brought a halt to the infection which had nearly rendered him blind.

Macular degeneration was a problem too, but seen as a normal part of old age. With the development of free eye-care, more and more people were using glasses, especially for reading – and this gave a boost to some of the patients.

I really enjoyed working on the male geriatric ward. It was interesting and I was able to get to know and empathise with the patients, which they seemed to appreciate.

When a death occurred, as it often did, we pulled the curtains, or screens, around the bed and washed the body, trying to make it presentable for the relatives. There was always the greatest respect for the departed patient and the grieving relatives. Although every death was a sad event, at least we knew we had done our best to make the patient's stay in the ward as comfortable and positive as possible. One can't do more.

~

One of the things I liked about UCH was the tunnels linking the nurses' home, the private patients wing, the main hospital and the maternity hospital. We were also able to get underground to University College, where they had student hops and activities of all kinds.

The hospital had been built in the shape of a Maltese cross and seemed enormous as there were four extensions which housed many of the clinics, wards and outpatient departments. In spite of its size, wherever I walked I always seemed to bump into the night sister. She was a dragon of a woman and terrified most of the junior staff, including me.

We nurses were lucky to have a good relationship with the chefs in the vast basement kitchens, and, if we could manage to vault over the iron railings surrounding the hospital, we could get to the steps leading down to where all kinds of goodies were cooking. This relationship also allowed us to get through a back corridor to the nurses' home, without being caught.

The Night Sister wasn't the only danger. I broke a front tooth on one of the railings when I slipped in the act of throwing my legs over a gate, in a vaulting-style of which I was rather proud, but caused me to gain my first false tooth.

One of the nights I went to the basement there was nobody around and, when I went into the kitchen, the ranges were teeming with cockroaches. It looked as if the whole cookers were moving. These enormously resilient insects looked like miniature tanks, ready to do battle. I learned later that they are one of the few creatures that could survive an atomic war and radioactive fallout. Certainly they seemed to thrive in the heat down there, but I did wonder where they all hid during the day. Heaven knows what modern health and safety committees would make of them.

One October, when the nights were beginning to draw in and winter began to encroach, we heard the dreaded air-raid siren. It always sent a shiver up my spine and brought back memories of the blitz. However, this time there were no lurking German bombers, simply an unexploded bomb. It had been found at the side of Maples, a large store which sported an enormous stuffed bear at the front entrance. Groups of medical students would often take the bear from its plinth and, with great ceremony, put it onto a truck, which sported flags and students waving pints of beer.

The bomb-disposal squad went to work and we had had to evacuate patients from the wards most at risk. Some of patients seemed quite pleased when the press printed their photos in the daily paper. It made their day, so something good came out of it.

The bear remained in place until the next rag day when it was driven along Tottenham Court Road and Oxford Street in an effort to raise funds for worthwhile causes.

~

One Christmas at UCH was quite an experience. Three other nurses and myself, working on a male medical ward, thought we ought to do something to celebrate and make life more enjoyable for those patients who couldn't go home.

We decided to take ourselves to Covent Garden where we could get fruit and vegetables for next to nothing. We arrived, in our uniforms, at five a.m. just when the main trading was taking place. There were numerous buyers and wholesalers selling all kinds of things. They only had to see our uniforms to give us whatever they could, even calling out to us and asking what we wanted. They wouldn't take a penny and we ended up with so much food that we couldn't carry it back to the hospital. We didn't have any money for a taxi, so they lent us an old wheelbarrow. We were grateful and promised to take it back as soon as we could.

We took it in turns to wheel our spoils through the morning traffic and back to the hospital. We used side streets in an attempt to miss the main flow. When at last we arrived, the patients were thrilled as we wheeled the barrow through the ward. Sadly for me, the other three nurses were due to go on duty. I was the only one on a late shift and had to push the wheelbarrow back to Covent Garden alone, trying not to notice the strange stares I received.

We had a wonderful day. One of the consultants dressed up as Father Christmas and took presents to the Children's wards. He returned and distributed all the goodies we had collected in Covent Garden, giving them to the patients and their visitors. In all, it was a wonderful example of the goodness and generosity of the people of London who, with their humour and passion, created a lovely atmosphere at a time when we were still experiencing rationing and limited availability of any kind of food.

When I went on duty I was asked to give one of our male patients a full bath. He had been in the ward for some time and had only just recovered from an operation after a difficult diagnosis. He was sick to death of blanket baths and wanted to soak in warm water to soothe his frayed nerves.

He was a very senior-ranking man from the Forces, as well as having been knighted for his war efforts. I have to say I was a bit nervous in case I did anything wrong. Helping him out of his dressing gown, I held out my hand to assist him into the bath. He sank down, still holding my hand, looked up at me, wriggled around and said, "Look nurse it floats".

Feeling a blush rising fast and furious I retrieved my hand, gave him the soap and flannel and told him to call me when he was ready to get out.

I had to laugh as his face was a picture. He reminded me of a saucy little boy. He did me a great favour because I learned that whatever social status, age or experience a man had, he was always the victim of his biology, anatomy and physiology.

~

My training required me to experience working with infectious diseases. This meant an allocation to either the Skin, or the TB ward. I was interested in both, but somewhat nervous of TB.

The TB epidemic in Britain was known as the "White Plague" and flourished among people with weak immune systems, especially those living in conditions of poor

26

sanitation and poverty, or who were malnourished. These were exactly the conditions found in many parts of London after WW2. There were vast areas, especially around the East End, where houses had been demolished by ceaseless bombing. People had lost their homes and the neighbourly connections upon which they depended.

TB was highly contagious and difficult to treat. It can survive outside a host for 88 days or more. It was thought at one time that European civilisation might be destroyed by it. At the turn of the century an estimated 50 million died from it every year, worldwide. London and New York were two of the worst affected cities.

My fear diminished when I arrived on the ward. I hadn't realised how much research was going on to deal with what had been the scourge of men women and children for so many years.

All members of staff who were working with pulmonary TB patients had to be immunised.

Streptomycin and Para-Amino-Salicylic (PAS), given together, were effective in treating the disease.

When I arrived on my first morning, only one woman looked up and smiled. Large gas cylinders fed oxygen to two patients. Several women were propped up in their beds and each had a sputum mug placed within easy reach.

The nature of the disease caused the coughing up of frothy sputum. Sometimes a coughing fit would result in large amounts of blood being brought up with inevitable distress to the patient. Of all infections, this one seemed to be the most debilitating. Nursing care meant complete rest for the patient, in order to help them recover sufficiently to return home, no longer infectious, to their families.

Many TB sufferers were sent to sanatoriums in the country where there was fresh air – thick smogs still happened in London. A lot of the patients had spent many months away from their families and this caused disruption and misery, especially if a mother had to leave her children in the hands of another family member, neighbours, or in some cases, a family volunteering through the church.

The routine was fairly similar to other wards. The day shift started at 7.30 a.m. Before the night nurses finished their shift we helped them wash the patients. Then we had to serve the breakfasts. I was asked on that first morning to make porridge. I wondered why there weren't any ward maids to do it, and never found out why. However, the porridge turned out OK, mainly because I had been used to making it for my father pretty well every day as he thought it healthy.

After breakfast, there were blanket-baths for the patients too ill to help themselves. Beds needed changing, and we attended to pressure points. There were also dressings to apply. Sputum mugs were removed for cleaning, each one had the bed number on it and was never given to another patient.

Every week, a sputum test was carried out to ascertain if the bacteria were still active.

If there was a doctor's round, the Sister made certain that all patients had their treatment beforehand. She also made certain that the patient's records such as temperature, respiration and blood pressure readings were recorded to inform the doctor about the progress of the disease. Bedpan and toilet rounds took place before and after every meal.

One patient, Mrs Morgan (Lily) was a pleasant woman. Her pale face used to peer above the sheets and she crunched them up in her hands as if they were trying to escape. She had four children, and her husband was trying to cope with the situation at home, a damp prefabricated house near the docks.

These houses, Prefabs, were often concrete slabs on

wooden frames, erected towards the end of the war to house the displaced population. Four walls, clamped together and joined to another four walls, became a permanent home to many families.

Lily preferred to be called by her first name, "It makes me feel more like myself and not stuck in a bed away from my kids". She often looked at me as if I was about to give her good news about her returning home. Sometimes she'd say something like, "I just want to get out of this place, nurse. My lovely children will be grown up before I can go home. I don't suppose they'll recognise me". She started to sob, which was one of the last things she should have done as the erratic flow of air caused stress on her lungs.

I said, "Why don't we ask Sister to speak to the doctor to see if one or two of them could poke their heads around the door one visiting day?". I felt sorry for Lily, as she had been in hospital for two months, although at that time it wasn't unusual for patients to be in care for much longer.

Many pulmonary TB patients had been incarcerated in sanatoriums, far from the dust and pollution of the city, as part of the effort to contain the disease, and far from their families.

The use of new medication brought salvation to so many people. New drugs had been developed to treat TB, and along with mass vaccinations and immunisations, the disease was being eradicated in the UK, especially in the cities where it had been rampant. That meant that Lily was probably going to be cured of the disease that had brought terror, suffering and bereavement to so many people.

Not only were human beings infected by the bacteria, but also animals. Cows in particular, if infected, could pass it on in the milk they produced. TB could affect other parts of the human body, especially bone formation. Pasteurisation, to kill the bacteria, was made compulsory, which meant all milk had to be brought to a high temperature before sale to the public.

It is unfortunate, but I suppose inevitable, that a bacteria which has been around for thousands of years, will return where conditions of poverty, malnourishment and poor immunity prevail – and it is on the rise in some parts of the world.

Lily was one of the last patients to be nursed in the TB ward, which was closed, along with many others, as the disease was effectively controlled. The doctor allowed her children to visit, but to stay outside the ward and peek through the open doorway. It was another two months before she was allowed home with strict advice on stress, good diet and to avoid putting strain on her lungs.

Some women on the ward had suffered enormously, not only from the disease, but also from the isolation from their families. I didn't hear that it was the cause of families being broken up permanently, as there was much greater social pressure for families to stay together than there is today.

Working on that ward was an experience I wouldn't have missed. It made me wish that the human race could be able to survive without fear of disease.

These days people are spared the horror of watching a TB victim coughing up frightening amounts of blood, as if they are bringing up their very lungs. It is a horrible disease and one which I hope will never return.

~

It was a dream come true when I looked at our notice board and saw the next list of placements. I was to spend three months on the Premature baby ward in the maternity hospital.

This was a separate building to UCH, on the other side of

the road. It came under the jurisdiction of the UCH Matron, but there were very senior Sisters there who had overall authority.

It was not particularly popular among the physicians, mainly because there didn't seem to be much for them to do. They stayed in the background, available but not often needed. There were a few procedures which the doctors performed such as setting up a transfusion for anaemia, or jaundice and naso-gastric tubes for feeding. The nurses were extremely competent and it was their skills that saved the infants' lives.

The basic care centred on warmth, watching for apnoea (absence of breathing), feeding and hygiene.

The unit had about twelve cots. Most babies would lie quietly, not ready to take an interest in the world. Some were wrapped in swaddling blankets or sheets.

It was thought that premature babies needed to feel secure, so their arms were wrapped into the sheet and the bottom part brought round to the back to keep it all tight.

Now it would be totally impossible to do that with the number of catheters and infusions attached to a poorly premature baby. However, the thing that hasn't changed is the need for total care. They required careful handling, avoidance of any infection and good record-keeping so that every person involved in their care knew exactly what the situation was with each baby.

It was crucial that they were fed correctly, and if the mother was available, breast milk was expressed for the baby. Women used to come to the hospital to do this and hand in the expressed milk. Mother's milk was thought to be so important that a milk-bank was set up so that no baby had to have artificial milk.

The cots in the premature baby unit were designed so that the ends could be raised or lowered, depending upon the baby's condition. In the case of respiratory difficulty the head end was placed higher to assist breathing. At that time it was thought that pure oxygen would be beneficial to the neonate. Unfortunately it was later found that some 10% of those babies suffered from retrolental fibroplasia as a result. This was the formation of fibrous tissue behind the lens of the eye and caused blindness. Once this was discovered we quickly changed the concentration given. However, those babies affected at that time spent the rest of their lives either blind, or only partially sighted.

We also used to promote respiration using steam from a kettle. This helped to moisten the air around the baby to improve shallow or laboured breathing.

It was unfortunate that the mortality rate was in the region of 30%, but as knowledge and skills grew it fell to 12%. Referrals from doctors and other people improved; the population became aware that treatment could help premature babies survive.

I remember when we had our smallest baby in the unit. It was about 1951 and this tiny bundle of humanity was brought in and placed in one of the cots. He weighed 15ounces, (425 grammes) just under a pound in weight. He was a dear little fellow, very pink and very distressed, but unaware of the world around him. I was sorely tempted to pick him up and give him a cuddle, but that wouldn't have been wise.

It seemed such a tragedy that he died. Our facilities at that time just weren't adequate; today he might well have survived.

In the last two months of pregnancy the brain develops greatly. Unless the nourishment and care is as good as the environment of the uterus before birth, it is possible for problems to develop.

Prematurity often led to the development of handicaps.

The incidence was about 10% at one time, having come down from a year or so before, when there wasn't the care available. However, as drugs and techniques developed, the incidence of handicaps dropped and survival rates improved. Causes of death were mainly listed as prematurity, intercranial haemorrhage, foetal deformity and infection.

I remember one huge woman approaching me, and saying, "How is little Alex getting on?" This woman was the mother of one of the tiniest, wrinkled little babies in the unit. He was hardly able to cry, being so weak. I made certain she had gowned up, and took her into the unit where her baby was silent in his cot. Tears came into her eyes and she said, "If anything happens to him I don't know what I'll do".

I replied, "He's a little fighter, we can only hope he manages to hold on. What about you? How are you dealing with everything?"

Alex's mother told me she had been diagnosed as a diabetic and had insulin injections every day. It had been difficult to stabilise her condition during her pregnancy, and she had suffered several hyperglycaemic episodes. I'm fairly certain her diabetes created problems for little Alex. Fortunately he did survive, but I was unable to follow his progress as I was allocated to another ward before he was discharged.

The one thing I really hated was feeding some of the babies by gastric tube. Passing a rubber tube down a tiny throat was scary and I used to worry that it would go into the lungs instead of the stomach. The thought of passing even a teaspoon of milk into a baby's lungs wasn't very cheering. However, I was taught to listen to the sounds at the end of the tube: if it was in the lungs one could hear breathing, however faint. Perhaps it was primitive, but it worked.

This was the first premature baby unit in London to have what was called a "Flying Squad" consisting of ambulance and staff.

We could be called out at any time of the day or night, carrying the equipment necessary for collecting a pre-term baby and returning to the hospital quickly.

The police would control traffic lights as we made our way from the pick-up point back to the unit, so there was never the risk of a driver having to brake hard and damage the baby. As soon as a call came through, we placed hot water bottles in pockets around the cot so that the baby would be kept warm. There was no temperature control other than checking the bottles and baby regularly.

The crew would drive as quickly as possible through the traffic, the siren clearing the way ahead.

Going out with the Flying Squad was an eye-opener for me. It was the first time I had been into some of the homes in the East End and I was full of admiration at the stoicism of the many women facing great hardship in that area.

Men also had a difficult time. More children added to a husband's difficulties; their responsibilities were enormous, yet most took it in their stride.

It may have been this experience of the community that eased me into joining the Queen's District Nursing team after I had finished my training at UCH.

~

The maternity ward at UCH was all hustle and bustle...

One patient, who was unable to speak or understand English, had just reached the final stages of labour. Our usual procedure was to take the patient by lift in a wheelchair to the delivery room on the next floor. She was very distressed as she couldn't understand what was happening and there was no one we could contact to interpret. I felt so sorry for her, but it was necessary to get her upstairs quickly so that she could benefit from gas and air to relieve the pain of her contractions. I wheeled her to the lift and pressed the call button, nothing happened. I pressed it again. This happened about five times and things were getting desperate. Near to the patient lift was the one used by the kitchen to take food to the wards. It was only the height of the food trolley, but in desperation I pressed the call button. When it arrived I ducked my head and pushed the patient and the wheelchair in, pressed the button for the next floor and, as we were in darkness, held the patient's hand to let her know I was there.

The patient had reached desperation point and was calling out "Anna, Anna". As luck would have it the lift went up to the next floor, but before I could get her out, it went back down again. It was nightmare for both the patient and myself, however she did arrive in the right place in time and delivered her lovely baby. I truly had visions of having to deliver the baby in the food-lift in the dark. It was an experience for both the patient and for myself and I think it was the start of my hair turning grey.

One morning the sister told me to stay by the door and not allow a certain patient, who was due to go home, to leave the ward without her baby. After a short time, the woman came to the door with her bag of bedclothes. She was an attractive woman with blonde hair down to her shoulders. Her black-skinned baby wasn't in sight and I asked where he was. She said she would collect him later and that he had been an accident. All she had done was to sit in the same bathwater as her lodger, consequently becoming pregnant with his child.

The woman was already married to a man who wouldn't take kindly to bringing up another man's child who was obviously not his own. I felt sorry for her; life isn't forgiving for those extra-marital mistakes one might have.

~

One morning I went on duty full of life, having had a good evening with a group of friends, some of whom were contemplating getting into a more serious relationship with their current boyfriends. It had been a wonderful evening, full of anticipation as to what the future was going to be.

I was a bit of an odd one out as I had several friends who were men, but I didn't look on any of them as possible suitors. I was just interested in having a good time and endeavouring to learn about life and coping with the shocks and surprises with as much common sense as possible.

One such shock was waiting for me as I went into the women's surgical ward that morning. There in the bed next to the sister's office was a lovely-looking girl who was covered with plaster from her neck to just below her hips. Her legs were in traction and her right lower arm was also plastered. A urinary catheter disappeared into a container at the side of the bed. With all this she could hardly move.

Beside her was a mug, with a spout, but unless a nurse helped her she was unable to drink.

As I approached the girl she looked at my eyes and I smiled, hoping my face didn't register the dismay I felt at her predicament. It was a wonderful moment though, because we made emotional contact.

I went into the office for the day's briefing. In these hand-overs we discussed new patients, changes in treatment or medication, the list of patients due for surgery and their preparation needs.

On this day the Sister could see I was upset. She was a very perceptive woman and kept me in her office when the other nurses had gone. She told me the girl was Asian and the unhappy bride in an arranged marriage. She hadn't even met her husband until the ceremony, but went through the process as required of her. It so happened that she realised she hated the man on sight and when the time came for him to claim what he thought were his rights in marriage, she broke away from him, jumped out of an open window and fell to the unforgiving ground. She had broken her spine in two places, dislocated her shoulder and broken the ulna and radius in an effort to break her fall.

The reason she had been placed next to the sister's office was that it was usually busy with consultants, doctors, students, nurses and ancillary staff. Any visitors she had could be closely monitored. Her father was furious that his arrangements had been ruined and his honour was in jeopardy. He had threatened to kill her, and the nurses felt the need to protect her.

It was all so very sad and it reminded me of the time in PTS when we were warned about the different ethical attitudes and lifestyles we would come across in our multicultural society. We learned of behaviours not allowed in our own culture, including the deliberate killing of female babies.

We certainly had to grow up when working at UCH, and try to take the world for what it is, good, dubious and bad.

The little Asian girl, who was all of fifteen years of age, made progress physically, but it wasn't certain how her injuries would affect the rest of her life. She stayed in hospital for several months and was discharged to stay with a relative who, under the eyes of the Almoner, looked after her.

~

Night duty in Casualty, at UCH, was always inundated with people who had nowhere to go, were suffering from the cold, malnourishment, or drunkenness. We had to be very careful that we didn't send somebody, who truly needed treatment in casualty, to Rowton House, St Martins in the Field, or another institution that provided for the homeless. There were those who just came in the hope of spending the night in one of our many cubicles, but we had to retain those for medical and surgical emergencies.

We knew that some of the people we recommended go to doss-houses etc. would end up bedding down in doorways, under the bridges that spanned the roads around Waterloo, St Pancras or Euston Station. Failing that, they might join the wino (meths-drinkers), who slept rough in bomb-sites. Of all of the options, Rowton House was way ahead in comfort and safety.

Rowton House had become the salvation of many working and non-working men. It also gave shelter to the significant numbers of Irish and other immigrants who had entered this country during and after the war to make a new life for themselves. Lord Rowton financed most of this institution, he also oversaw the furnishing and running of it. He had even taken one of the beds back home with him in order to test it for suitability. His reputation of being a great philanthropist was truly justified, and he provided undreamed-of luxury to thousands of men who were living their lives at a low ebb.

It may be remembered that George Orwell wrote a book called "Down and Out in London and Paris". He actually tested out Rowton House and although he was impressed, he stated that the buildings would still be called doss-houses.

Victorian attitudes to drink, gambling and playing cards, were applied in these institutions, and a fine was payable if any of the men were incontinent.

With such a mix of people using the facilities available it was necessary to impose an acceptable form of behaviour, and although sometimes the inevitable fight broke out it was soon dealt with. Most of the Rowton House buildings remain and possibly may still be in use.

Apart from these men hoping for a good night's sleep, there were genuine patients. Fireworks Night in casualty was a particularly interesting experience. It always amazed me how few people thought about the dangers of burning an effigy of Guy Fawkes, or of fireworks and bonfires. With shrieks of laughter and enjoyment, children would watch as various parts of the guy stuffed with straw or paper, complete with some kind of mask or painted face, topped with a hat, would burst into flames, illuminating the world around.

There were the bangs and flares of fireworks, crackers and jumping sizzlers, plus the inevitable sparklers that even the very young used to hold and wave around to make lighted patterns in the dark night.

Burns, scalds, seared flesh, clothes and hair having been on fire, were always a part of the scene.

Usually, two days or more before the big day, the children would search and find anything they could beg, borrow or steal to make a life-sized model of the fêted man. They used old clothes left over from a church sale, or anything too worn to wear. They often purloined an old pram, or a box from the greengrocers to which they fixed wheels. It was a great communal effort to outdo the guy made in the next street. Then, of course, the children didn't neglect the opportunity to earn a few pennies from all their efforts and would wheel their guy around the streets shouting "Penny for the guy". Most people gave a copper or two when asked. It was all in the spirit of the occasion.

It was about nine-thirty, that evening, when we heard a great rumpus coming towards Casualty from the slope leading down to it. One of the medical students and I looked at one another with the sort of expression that indicates, "Here we go".

Jack, a scruffy lad, was brought in by his friends. He was about ten years of age, had a voice better than the best town crier, and was hollering loud enough to wake people a mile away. He was all over the place stamping his feet and throwing himself about. His frightened companions took off as soon as they saw we were about to deal with him. It was obvious they wanted to take no responsibility for his condition. They disappeared into the increasingly smoky night, never to be seen by us again.

The medical student and I started to pull off his clothes and his wellington boots to find out what his problem was, and as his right wellington came off, a red hot firework, which had somehow entered his sock, fell out on to the floor. It had burnt his ankle and leg quite badly. We lifted him on to a trolley and put a soaking wet cold towel over the whole area. We replaced the cold water several times to cool the wound and reduce the damage. However, it was obvious that there was an area in the middle of the burn which was third degree – all layers of the skin having been burned. Elsewhere the damage was less serious, and the nerves hadn't been affected.

We spoke to the lad slowly and clearly so that he had time to collect his thoughts and calm down. He told us that he and his friends had been challenged by another group of boys and the two gangs threw lighted fireworks at one another. It wasn't uncommon for some lads to take things to these extremes. I gave him some sips of water and his pain eventually became bearable.

A new dressing, tulle gras, came to our aid. We cleansed the area and placed the tulle over the wound, finishing with some padding and bandage. I arranged for Jack to come back to the Outpatients clinic two days later, or the following day if he was in too much pain.

We couldn't put the boot over the wound, so we lent him a pair of plimsolls. Fortunately he lived only a short distance away. He did come back to the Outpatients department, but we didn't see the plimsolls again. Perhaps he forgot, or liked them better than his wellingtons.

~

As a nurse, I met all types of people, from prostitutes to great politicians. During my time in the private patients wing at UCH, I nursed Herbert Morrison's wife, and found the couple to be most congenial. In spite of losing the sight of one eye due to an infection as a child, Herbert Morrison managed very well with monocular vision. He had left school at the age of sixteen, starting out as an errand boy until he joined the Independent Labour Party. It was his humble beginnings and a clear idea of the lot of the commoner in London, that gave him the impetus to rise through Labour Party ranks and become a powerful force in the government's efforts to improve conditions for the general public.

He is quoted as saying, "Wealth is no longer the passport to the best health treatment," and the National Health Service became the salvation of many underprivileged people. He was also one of the few politicians then who had had no money to start his career.

The Londoners thought of him as a beneficent uncle who had their welfare at heart. To improve the terrible conditions in the East End, and especially Hackney, where he had become mayor, he wrote the blueprint for nationalisation and the welfare state. Earlier, as leader of the London County Council, he had become responsible for air raid precautions and the National Fire Service. He also oversaw the development of London's housing, health, education and transport systems.

He designed the Morrison bomb-shelters that helped to save many lives in the East End. There were two types of shelter, the Morrison's and the Anderson's. These were made of corrugated iron parts which were pre-formed for people to erect in their gardens. Most people dug a hole to place the shelter as low down in the ground as possible to give extra protection. Some families slept in them every night just to feel safer and be able to sleep undisturbed. Others slept in the underground stations, deep beneath the streets of London. The platforms used to be covered with all kinds of bedding until the first trains arrived in the early morning carrying workers. Then there was a mass exodus and people returned home.

I feel that Herbert Morrison isn't remembered with the gratitude he deserves. Though he was knighted, so are many people. He was a great man whose dedication to mankind and to the reduction of suffering was exceptional.

~

Another patient I was enchanted to meet was Wendy Toye, someone I admired and came to love. We became friends in our long discussions during her treatments in the private patients' wing.

Until her hospitalisation she had been the choreographer for some of the shows at the London Palladium, where the famous Tiller girls performed with such perfect timing. These girls, so carefully chosen for their height, performance and vivacity, were the talk of London. It was Wendy who was instrumental in helping to get everything right in order to cram the Palladium every week with all kinds of people wanting to see the show. The costumes used were similar to those of the Follies Bergere and therefore eye-catching and impressive. They always seemed to have huge feathers on their heads which draped and swayed as the dancers moved and did their high kicks in synchrony.

Wendy occupied a side room and was on dialysis for kidney failure. At first she didn't look particularly ill, but as the weeks went by she began to show the severity of her condition. She developed rings round her eyes. They looked abnormally dark in a face which was slowly becoming drawn and exhausted. She was always eager to have a chat as I made her bed and sorted out the various catheters to which she had been attached.

She was such a lovely person who, I believed, was living too early in time to be saved. Her kidneys were giving up and the poisons in her body were slowly but assuredly killing her. Now we have the know-how to deal with these conditions more effectively.

Making my way to the private patients' wing, one morning, I felt happy that the nights were getting lighter and there was the beginning of Spring around the corner. It was a sunny day, and I looked forward to seeing Wendy and telling her about the write-up of the show I had seen in the paper. Entering her room, the first things I felt were the emptiness and a desolate feeling of loss; then I saw the empty bed. I looked in the bathroom, half-knowing that she wouldn't be there. It is only sixty years later that my assiduous editor discovered Wendy hadn't died in the night as I had thought. The night staff had cleared everything away to move her to intensive care. There was nothing left of her that I could hold or see. Nobody informed me where she was, and I assumed she had died. Now however I feel so pleased that she managed to conquer her illness and continue with the colourful and exciting theatre work that she so loved. She became one of the first female film directors and was involved in several popular and well-known films until her death in 2010. My memory of her is now much happier, and I'm sure she gave much pleasure to many theatre-goers.

These things all add up to experience I suppose, but it did make me realise how fleeting life can be.

~

Those old enough to remember one or two well-known film stars such as James Mason and Margaret Lockwood may recall Tyrone Power. He made many films in America and in England, and was, to me, a gift to mankind. In fact I almost saw him as the perfect man. He was handsome, seemingly without being self-opinionated, abusive or violent, and his smile made the sun shine.

I wasn't at that time too aware that he was merely acting, and I admit to having had a crush on him.

It was whilst working in the private patients' wing that the sister in charge told me we were admitting a new patient and we had to make the preparations for him. He was due to have an operation the following morning and there were certain procedures to follow.

It didn't mean much to me, but I did perk up when I found out it was none other than Tyrone Power, and I was thrilled at the thought of meeting him.

It is said about life that everything depends on the way you interpret things, and the assumptions you carry around with you. Tyrone Power was much diminished in my eyes after I learnt of the abusive way he had treated the reporters outside the hospital, the nature of his operation (a haemorrhoidectomy) and the fact that he was height-challenged. It was apparently well-known that he had to have (insisted on) a stool the height of which would raise him to match that of his co-star. He had his shoes especially made with raisers in to give him height. During his stay in the ward he turned out to be a good example of the short bully who needs to feed his ego.

This was a bit too much for my young mind as it brought home the artificiality of the film industry. At one time one could say, "Seeing is believing", and the film industry has embraced this, changing anything to that which is conducive to bringing in dollars.

Like many others, he came, had his operation and left without too many people getting involved. It was just like any other week and we went on as before. He was discharged minus haemorrhoids and admiration.

~

And so I came towards the completion of the three-year training. For various reasons, not all of our set finished. One of those that left, Isobel, was a fellow student, a personal friend and lovely company. She never seemed to get involved or friendly with anybody other than me.

Her mannerisms and body language were charming, but exaggerated, waving her hands, as if to wash away an unpleasant thought, or tilting her face to the sky as if momentarily deep in thought. I had never seen a smile so wide as hers.

She struggled with the training and I suspected she'd had too little preparation to cope with the vast range of people and stresses student nurses had to deal with on a day-to-day basis. I often wondered what niche in life would suit her better. I felt sorry for Isobel and I have always been a soft touch for anybody who needed support.

As the training progressed, problems mounted for some students. Poor Isobel, with her clumsy movements, sometimes got into a mess, such as spilling water all over a patient and the floor when filling a jug.

In the operating theatre, her regular knocking over trays of sterile instruments led to a decision by the senior sister that her talents would be best served elsewhere.

It was with great trepidation she delivered herself to Matron's office when asked to do so by the senior Sister of the theatre department. Isobel stood outside the door with that well-practised smile on her face.

Off-duty, she was great company, and made me laugh when she went to extraordinary lengths to attract males of any colour or age—and there were many attracted to her.

Coming off duty, she would put on the brightest red lipstick and shake her head to loosen her long, dark hair, which had been tied up and hidden within the statutory white, starched cap of our uniform.

Isobel was her own worst enemy when choosing clothes. She had little idea of fashion and bought herself a very wide belt, which she fastened round her waist and tightened to her goal of eighteen inches. This left a considerable bulge above and below her waist.

She was acutely conscious of effect she had on men, but hopelessly naïve, and, complete with crimson lips and long locks, landed herself in situations from which she often needed rescuing with my assistance.

I suspect she took her caring instincts too far with some men, and may have been seen as "The Good Samaritan of Tottenham Court Road".

Isobel eventually abandoned her training and left the hospital. I have a feeling the senior Sisters breathed a sigh of relief when they last saw her swaying backside disappear towards Warren Street underground station.

Isobel and I kept in touch. She lived in Darlington, and I caught the train to go and stay with her for a weekend. It was a sunny day when I arrived, after a week of rain and dark clouds, and heralded a lovely weekend.

Arriving at her address and knocking at the door, I heard an infant snuffling. Isobel let me in, while holding a baby about one-month old. She was as proud of her child as any mother I have ever seen, and it was a joy to see her cuddling him, singing songs and tucking him up in his cot, a sturdy, wooden drawer placed on the floor. There was no sign of any father and I didn't feel it tactful to ask questions.

Isobel was happy, her clumsiness had vanished, only to be replaced with an easy confidence, and there was clearly no danger of her dropping the baby.

She spent most of the time telling me about him, his feeds, his sleeping pattern, and the way he clenched his fists when hungry. She managed to breast-feed him without problems and was extremely proud of it.

It was good to see Isobel so content. Her father lived nearby and I learned he was proud to be a grandfather, something he'd really looked forward to.

With a whole new image of Isobel, I returned to London. She had found her niche and, with her father's support, was coping well with life.

~

The final examinations for the qualification of State Registration involved written papers and practical examinations. We were informed of an entrance fee we had to pay when we applied to take the exam.

At that time our monthly salary was seven pounds, and most of that went on the usual toiletries, food and some scant make-up.

The meals we were given in the nurses' home was the same mass-cooked food supplied to the patients in the wards. The patients were relatively lucky, because they were normally in hospital for a limited time; relatives and friends also brought in all kinds of goodies for them to eat.

We nurses, on the other hand, had to make do with what we were served, and although the chefs meant well, the food was predictable and fairly boring. Sometimes we spent our meagre wage on something more palatable.

So it was that my friend and myself, were skint and didn't know where to find the fees for our exam. Neither of us would have stooped to asking our parents for anything, let alone money, so we were in a pickle.

It was one of the nurses in the set above us who told us what several of her group had done. They had visited a pawnbroker to raise enough for the exam fee. She gave us an address in Camden Lock, near the Sunday market.

Neither of us had much of an idea as to what we should pawn, but I took my fob watch. It was the one I used when taking a patient's pulse. My colleague took a watch her father had given her. She was unable to buy it back and never forgave herself.

Armed with our little parcels we caught the bus to Camden Lock and easily found the shop. One couldn't miss it; three giant balls hung outside to indicate its nature.

We both tried to be invisible as we opened the door, but a very pleasant man smiled and approached us. It was almost as if he knew what we needed and why. My guess was that many nurses such as ourselves had made use of his services.

Here was a man with two opposing ambitions. One was to make money and the other was to appease his conscience. He seemed to be a really nice chap.

He showed us some of the things people had brought in and he kept them all safely stored away from thieving hands for three months. If they weren't reclaimed after that time, he used to take them up to Portobello Road and sell them, making certain he made a reasonable profit.

Many people never returned to buy their pawned goods

back, although in Canning Town, very often the best shoes of the head of household were pawned for buying food and bought back again after pay day which was normally Friday afternoon, just in time for him to go out to enjoy his pint with his mates at the pub. I had a suspicion that many men had no idea how much of their clothing was in the possession of pawnbrokers, due to their wife's efforts to make ends meet and put food on the table.

My parents never knew what I had done. Neither did they know I had once walked all the way through Blackwall Tunnel amongst the traffic because I didn't have enough to pay for a bus. It all comes down to pride I suppose, but this is how we maintained our self-esteem and dignity in those days.

The following day my friend and I went to Matron's office and handed in the money. The Sister Tutor checked that all was well and we went off like two conspirators, having succeeded in our little subterfuge.

~

I felt like a totally different person in my third year at the hospital. I'd come across so many different people and learned a lot about what it is to be a human. There had been people from many walks of life, religions and with very different values.

Our performance had been assessed in every ward or section to which we had been allocated during our training. Any nurse failing to come up to standard was either given extra help, or eased out.

I remember one student nurse who went round her ward with a bowl, telling people to put their false teeth in so that she could clean them all. I still wonder if everybody got the right teeth back. Dentures were very common in those days and most people had an upper or lower set, or even both.

I marked every day off on the calendar as the SRN examination day came closer. I think most of us developed nerves and felt the urgency to swat up on not only anatomy, physiology and biology, but also different tests and procedures, hygiene, nutrition and hospital ethics.

Our group discussed the forthcoming exam and we all wondered what we would do if we failed, or if we passed, and whether we would stay on another year to take the hospital diploma.

I found these repetitive and emotional discussions too much, so I often made certain I was too busy and not available for them.

I was tempted by the idea of going over to work in the American hospital in Paris as Paris was a city I loved. Instead, I chose to stay on and take the diploma. I had a very deep affection for UCH and everything it stood for. I admired the people there; we were like a very big family.

Waiting for exam results was always gruelling. Some mornings I would be optimistic and think "Of course I've passed"; on others I would feel that it would be too good to be true.

The exam itself hadn't been quite as difficult as I had envisaged. The practical assessment involved several examiners experienced in different specialities asking me to demonstrate techniques and procedures.

The written exam came in two parts. One paper was more theoretical, but the other was very difficult for me, testing my ability to work out strategies for potential situations I might face while in charge of a ward.

I can't remember how long it took to receive the results, but when they came I felt I had been crowned queen.

The feeling of succcess and achievement was overpowering, and more than ever I realised I had made the right choice for my life.

The Sister Tutors came and congratulated us all. They were keen to enjoy our success and celebrated with us in the nurses' home that evening. One of the senior tutors became decidedly tipsy, and I was pleased to see her happy, relaxed and informal. She was truly dedicated to a high standard of patient care, and it showed in the quality of the training she gave her students.

I t wasn't all work and no play. I loved being in London, the social life, the people and the culture. Lyons Corner Houses, for instance, were popular places to meet and eat. They had several different types of restaurant in each building, giving you plenty of choice. Often the Corner Houses were very busy, being the focus of much socialising in the popular parts of London.

I used to go to their 'Salad Bowls', which were normally in the basement. There was always a small group of musicians playing popular music.

One could go back time and again for more helpings and I was always amused to see the same faces appearing with a plate ready for a refill.

In one Corner House I met a practising prostitute. She was an anorexic-looking woman with badly applied make-up. Her mouth, thin and mean-looking, was lathered in crimson lipstick, which was as good as wearing a badge to announce her profession.

We fell into conversation when she was standing next to me, waiting for a table. She seemed pleased to talk to a stranger and offloaded some of the problems she was having in her life, not seeming to mind if anyone overheard what she was saying. I felt so privileged to be in London where you could meet all types of people and chat. Sometimes I never saw them again.

For this woman, making money was very important. Her family had been living in a rat-infested area near the London Hospital off Commercial Road. Her mother had severe asthma and blamed this on damp walls and the fumes from the never-ending traffic. The prostitute told me she had seen an old chap sitting on a bench for hours in the small park there, and found out later that he had been dead all that time. "It's all over for 'im though, love, innit? 'E's lucky, the rest of us 'as to put up wiv things."

I felt very sorry for her, but her being a prostitute was no great surprise to me, given the terrible circumstances in which many people lived.

Apart from the Corner Houses a favourite entertainment was music. I remember Edmundo Ross performing at the Lyceum ballroom. He was the first conductor of Latin-American music I had heard. A superb foot-tapper, he swayed his over-generous body to the music, making you want to get up and dance, as did Carmen Miranda, the dancer and singer, popular and well known for her ridiculous hat made of artificial fruit, and miraculously perched on her head whilst she gyrated to the music.

I also went to the Nuffield Club, a place specifically for men and women who were, or had been, in the Forces, though nurses were welcome too. It was here that the lads, sick of fighting and wanting some escape, came to savour the comradeship they found there.

A very popular pastime in London was greyhound racing. One of my patients, "Old Ted Waters", was a man with expertise in two things. Firstly, in spite of his gammy leg, injured when his house had collapsed in one of the air raids, he loved going to Walthamstow greyhound-racing stadium to try his hand at winning bets. He reckoned life owed him one for the way he had tolerated his wife, Ada, for forty years, and who had been famously known as the witch of Club Road.

Sometimes the pain he felt got the better of him and I used to go and apply various ointments and bandage his knee with thick elastic tape to reduce the inflammation, which flared up if he walked too much. Going up and down the steps of the stadium didn't help, but it was one of the two things he lived for.

His second hobby, another popular pastime in London, was breeding homing pigeons. In his back yard, there must have been at least twenty cages piled one on top of another. There was always a mess on the yard floor from droppings and spilled seed, something Ada used to scream at him about. "If you don't keep that bleedin' yard cleaner, Ted Waters, I'm leavin' you".

"Chance would be a bloody thing", Ted would mutter and raise his eyes to the sky in disgust. For all the aggro that Ada gave him, he did make a profit from his pigeons, as a good one could be worth quite a few pounds. He loved each one like they were his children, and if one of them didn't return from a flight, he was beside himself.

"Them birds is what I live for, nurse. They never moan an' groan like me bleeding wife. She'd make any man go on 'is 'ands and knees an' pray for a miracle." He suffered a great deal of pain, but took his full allowance of painkillers and soldiered on.

Boxing was a most popular sport in those days, and discussed just about anywhere. Some boxers were taken into the hearts of the Londoners. Dear old Freddie Mills was one who, having trained in the East End clubs, took part in many tournaments and, latterly, matches against fighters from abroad. He was a great favourite of mine as he gave the appearance of being a gentle giant. The media loved him, as did the sporting world, partly I suppose because he was such a familiar figure, but also because of his quiet sense of humour.

He appeared in one of the London pantomimes. Loud cheers went up when he walked on stage. He beamed back, his lovely black skin shining with perspiration – he'd been nervous about appearing before so many children.

I only watched him boxing once. Though there was the tension of the ring and the audience eager for action, I couldn't deal with the way men punched the daylights out of each other. It all seemed too brutal for me, but the men and some women enjoyed the spirit of the fight and the spectacle of the best man winning. There was also the consideration many had of winning their bets on the outcome. Certainly money changed hands rather rapidly, both overtly and covertly.

Freddie had the knack of grimacing a smile, as much as his gum shield allowed, whenever he managed to get up after a vicious punch from his opponent. Knowing a little more now about how things worked, perhaps most of it was just showmanship, but he certainly could throw a hefty punch that stunned opponents.

Freddie owned a nightclub in Charing Cross Road, which was both a good and bad thing for him. Good, because it gave him another dimension to his life, but bad, because he ran into debt. Both the Krays' and Richardson's gangs had their eyes on the club. Freddie was neither a good entrepreneur nor a match for those thugs, and both gangs wanted to take over his patch, which was in an excellent position in the middle of a great deal of night life.

My colleague, who was a medical student at UCH, suggested we gave the place a try and, as it was within reasonable walking distance, we made our way there to "test the water". We had to go down below street level to get to the action. There were the usual dimmed lights and waiters darting about to serve the clients.

We were given a table at the side of the chap playing the piano. The scene reminded me of the film Casablanca and the dark-skinned pianist who revealed a wonderful set of pearl-white teeth when he smiled. Certainly the food was good, taking into account that rationing was still ongoing. However, supplies were beginning to get easier and, at the club, I saw bananas for the first time. The main thing I enjoyed was the rum they sold there. It was the thick navy rum used at that time by the Merchant and Royal Navies and it wouldn't have surprised me if some of it hadn't been supplied through some shady deal with dock workers.

Sadly, the pressures heaped on Freddie Mills were too much for him. He became increasingly depressed as his debts grew and the actions of those who wanted to move in became intolerable.

One morning we woke up to the news that Freddie had shot himself while in his car. His gun was next to him and, as far as I know, there was no suspicion of anyone else involved. Many of my patients were extremely upset when they learned of his death. They had followed his boxing career, and somehow it had become personal and left them, and me, with an emptiness; a feeling of tragedy that never quite left.

~

There were close ties between U.C.H and University College, even to the extent of an underground tunnel between the two, as there was between the Maternity Hospital and the Private Patients Wing.

There were many social events in the university and we nurses were often invited to dances, hops and just get-togethers. It was at one of these that I was introduced to a German student who was studying at the Slade School of Fine Art. He had been a prisoner of war, having been captured at the Russian Front where thousands were killed in terrible conditions. He came from Freiburg, a wonderful old University town and had worked on aircraft design before having to go into the German army.

Somehow we clicked and found ourselves on the same wavelength. He had a positive world view of life and a wicked sense of humour, which is so important for keeping things in perspective. Because of the possible problems of my marrying a former "enemy", we took ourselves off to a Registry Office and got married secretly.

When eventually we went to meet my parents, they took to Erich straight away, and I shall always be grateful to them for being so supportive.

Erich became an authority on the Bauhaus Movement and taught at the then well-known Hornsey College of Art, which later became part of North East London University. We were all so proud when one of Erich's sculptures was accepted by the Royal Academy. Later he taught History of Art at London University, having brought over from Germany the important exhibition "Sehen".

We became avid supporters of the Friends of the Tate, but I still carried on with my own interests of Nursing and Psychology.

Tragically, Erich's experiences in the terrible cold at the Russian Front were the reason that he, and many others who had the same experience, developed an enlarged heart. It was devastating for such a talented man and he died at fifty-four.

~

The East End of London was a magnet for those people wanting to escape from other lands and to have the benefits of living in a country which was generally supportive and non-aggressive.

On the whole this worked very well, but as with all things, once anything intruded too much on the fabric of the culture embedded for centuries, tensions could arise and were often difficult to deal with in a positive way.

Some people brought skills from their own countries. One of these was millinery, and one such immigrant had managed to set up shop as a hatter. If one looked in the shining window of the shop, with not a smudge to be seen on the glass, there, displayed with the utmost care, were hats of all sizes and colours, with ribbons and feathers adding panache for women with enough money to parade in their trips to church and for weddings, funerals and christenings.

It was unfortunate that this shop was not in a good

position trade-wise. It was just off Commercial Road in an area not altogether in the front-line of fashion. Having said that, the local women made great efforts to outdo one another at social gatherings, and my guess was that the local pawnshops had an increase of offerings when such an occasion was due.

One of my patients was friendly with the owner of the shop, who had escaped from persecution in her own country and was trying hard to adjust to a different culture.

Time and again her shop window was smashed by youths, who felt able to judge whether or not she and her husband were entitled to the house they were given, which went with the shop.

Intimidation grew to the point she was frightened to go out unless accompanied by her husband. He had good intentions, but had been given a job as a delivery man, and it wasn't always possible to be where his wife wanted him.

My patient, who suffered from an enlarged thyroid gland, which made her edgy and nervous, offered to do the shopping for the couple so that they weren't without food. She used to get a list from the woman, skirt round and do the shopping as best she could, and then make her way to the back of the house where there was an alleyway. Going through the yard, she used to knock on the window, which was opened for her to hand in the shopping. She was deeply upset when the couple left and all the hats disappeared from the shop.

These experiences were great insights into the workings of human behaviour, and left me wondering if we can really be blamed for anything we do, and whether we are victims of our own culture and doctrines.

~

Arthur (Art) and Sarah Gregg, Pearly King and Queen, were a lovely couple. They were true-blue East End cockneys and proud of it. They often spoke in the kind of language which had come about partly through humour, but also to communicate between members of their local group without being understood by outsiders.

Apart from the political and social philanthropists, who were keen to help the underclasses, it was obvious to these costermongers and labourers that the wealthy were not going to help them in any way.

This may be because the wealthy didn't understand how hard life was for those people living on the breadline and who stood little chance of getting out of it.

Because of this, the lower classes stuck together and helped each other. They knew what the score was and did what they could to make things as easy as possible for one another.

They were a tough crowd and didn't suffer fools gladly, but having said that, they would readily offer help to those who needed it.

Their philosophy was "Some you win, some you lose" and accepted failure when it happened. That was life; one got over disaster and moved on.

Art and Sarah had their own group of followers, and anybody in the area could join. I think the Pearly Kings and Queens were the first step towards trades unions. They were mainly involved in doing whatever was needed for the community. Their evenings at the local pub were wonderful times of bonding and shared lives. The men talked about greyhound racing, pigeon racing, boxing and, another popular pastime in post-war East London, rat-killing competitions.

I remember the women loved what they referred to as "a knees-up" and they would have a laugh about the knickers that came on show in the process. The Can-Can girls of the French shows in Paris, had nothing on the East End women when they danced. I look back in admiration at these people who bore hardships by having a wonderful camaraderie. I fell in love with them. The toothy grins, the hair in huge rollers, the weathered hands and faces, the raucous laughter, soft-capped men holding pints of beer, which disappeared as quickly as they were poured. These evenings were, to me, the essence of what real life was about.

The Kings and Queens wore clothes to which hundreds of pearl buttons had been stitched to jackets, trousers, skirts, hats and caps. They really stood out in a crowd. I was told that it had become a tradition from a young lad who was "down and out" and who collected buttons he found in the streets. He managed to sell some and gave everything he could to charity.

The Pearly Kings and Queens carried on this tradition and even now, sixty-odd years later, still get involved in special celebration days, where they collect for charity.

While I was working in Casualty, Art was brought in by the ambulance men one night. He had been at his local pub, enjoying an evening with the boys, when some sailors from one of the boats came in and started a fight. They had complained that the barman was too slow in serving them and gave the wrong change. Needless to say there was a good old punch-up, with chairs being used to try to calm things down, so we were told. Arthur had some good fists on him and I'm sure he gave as good as he received, but in the event he lost several teeth and dislocated his shoulder. Though he didn't want Sarah to know of this event, it was going to be difficult for him to grin or smile without her noticing the missing teeth and possibly knocking out a few more.

It didn't take long to reset his shoulder and put his arm in a sling to rest it, but we could only mop up the blood which had trickled down his face as a result of his teeth being extracted in such a violent way. We gave him a few codeine tablets to see him through the night. The ambulance men had long disappeared, but Art's friend offered to take him home on the bus. The nursing staff said goodbye to them and promised to go to one of their Pearly get-togethers.

~

I was troubled by the difficulties women faced at that time; the absence of much in the way of birth control put a great deal of responsibility on them, and they had to deal with it as best they could, using various techniques mostly handed down from their mothers, or as was frequently the case, using different methods to abort.

The use of douches was often fairly successful where the woman would give herself a douche of fairly strong vinegar. This was also used if a woman suspected the man of having a venereal disease. As far as aborting was concerned, there were two main methods. One was to have another woman to help insert a catheter into the uterus and syringe warm water in. Some women simply used a knitting needle and this pierced the plug usually in place protecting pregnancy.

Some women, whose beliefs were against any form of birth control, used the simple method of checking their temperature every day, ascertaining when they would be most fertile, and abstaining from sex on those days, but most women weren't in a position to do this, partly because of ignorance.

Marie Stopes clinics helped women to overcome their difficulties, and advice was free, but there was only one in London at that time. Marie Stopes was a great believer in the rights of women to have control over their own lives, and particularly their own body. The clinic in London was out of reach for many women in the East End and most were unable to able to use it. Now, however, there are clinics in many countries throughout the world and anyone can go for treatment or advice about anything relating to either male or female reproductive systems. They also deal with the various types of venereal disease, or sexually transmitted infections, STIs, as they are now called.

There was a great deal of ignorance then, and although pregnancy was often welcomed and seen as the natural order of things, it was a problem for many large families without proper accommodation, heating, enough food, and those in poor health. In a large family it was often the case that a baby might not survive beyond its first few days of life. Families struggling to make ends meet, on a small and unpredictable wage packet, often had a diminished immune system brought about by constant colds and poor food. The men who worked in the docks never knew if they would have work for the week, or even for a single day, because of the methods used for recruitment which were erratic and depended on relationships with gang-masters.

Often, if a mother found she was pregnant yet again, she would try to abort the foetus, sometimes by drinking Lysol, a powerful disinfectant, which often killed the mother and her foetus.

In these conditions it wasn't easy for women to deal with rebellious or sickly children. I usually found mothers in poor health and struggling to cope. I also had the job of dealing with the bruises and split lips of women with violent husbands.

One woman blamed her breast cancer on her husband; she accused him of pulling her around by her breasts when he had too much to drink.

One of the back street abortionists I knew of, charged two pounds to terminate a woman's pregnancy. Cleanliness was an issue. It was easy for infection to take hold, and I did try to educate abortionists to consider cleanliness in their work. It wasn't for me to be judgemental; my job was to promote health wherever possible.

One struggling family I visited was the Bradleys. They had three children of ten, eight and four. The ten-year-old was a girl, the others boys, however the two oldest children were handicapped. The girl, Ada, had spina bifida, which is a condition in which part of the spinal cord shows itself through, or between one of the vertebrae of the spinal column. The other child, Eddie, suffered from Down's syndrome, which meant he was of a lower educational standard due to an extra chromosome. The youngest son, little John, was very poorly with a constantly flowing nose and cough. His lungs always sounded dreadful, and I didn't have too many hopes for him surviving flu or measles.

They were dear little children with hardly the future that I could hope for them. Their parents were brother and sister living as husband and wife. Strangely, it wasn't thought to be a problem by any of the extended family.

The only time the Bradleys had seen a doctor was when

the girl was first born with spina bifida. She received surgery in a clinic attached to a workhouse.

Later, I came across the same kind of incest in very rural areas, but it was more often between father and daughter, and also led to family, social and genetic difficulties.

Childhood death was no stranger in these times and seen as just a part of life. It does make me realise how much the world has changed over the last sixty years.

Before the NHS was formed, seeing doctors cost money. If your illness merited it and you had the money to pay, you could get treatment. It was possible to pick up an infection in the doctor's own waiting room, especially tuberculosis and the infectious diseases of childhood, such as measles, mumps and rubella, all of which were controlled when vaccination and immunisation became available for free.

Almost overnight, it seemed, immunisation ended the scourge of polio and iron lungs were scrapped and relegated to history.

Several of the families I had to visit found life a constant struggle. It was a time when pawnshops were to be seen in many areas; however one had to have the things to pawn. One woman I knew pawned her son's coat and if it rained before she had any money to get it back the poor lad got soaked.

In many homes there would be a huge pot of stew bubbling away, and anything edible was thrown in and boiled. Sometimes this stock-pot was used for several days, and the original piece of meat would be joined by whatever was available.

With so many families on the bread-line at that time, cheap food was a priority. Some locals were forced to buy food intended for animal consumption, rather than the costlier meat fit for humans.

Bert was a man who led his old horse around the Poplar area and sold cat-food from his cart. He was given the title of "The Cats' Meat Man". Bert was a happy old soul who dribbled continuously down one side of his face in an effort to keep his full set of false teeth where they were meant to be. He was a familiar figure and gardeners used to follow his cart with a bucket and spade, collecting horse droppings to help vegetables grow in allotments.

Bert, like many of his kind, had suffered rickets when he was young, and his legs created an ovoid shape when he walked.

As far as I know, eating meat meant for cats didn't cause any harm, but staved off the hunger pangs of poverty-stricken people, many of whom had emigrated here to try to find a better life.

~

Many immigrants arrived on the boats that came in to East India Docks. Jews came over from Eastern Europe and set up clothing businesses wherever they could, a good few of them in Aldgate and around Petticoat Lane. More people arrived from Bangladesh and also from the Caribbean and West Africa, and London began to have a significant influx of those who were truly a different colour.

Prince Monolulu had jet-black skin, and used to be heard in Petticoat Lane shouting, "I gotta horse, I gotta horse." He wore huge feathers in his hair and sported colourful clothes, which made him stand out from the crowds. A lovely man who took bets on horses, he always had a huge, toothy smile for me, and in a loud voice said, "Lovely day, nurse," in good English. He was very popular with the police and I did sometimes wonder if they risked their hard-earned money backing his horses.

The Chinese kept to themselves at that time, and were often linked to the opium trade, or so the police told me. The Chinese had their own houses in the district of Limehouse, where I saw rooms lined with tiered bunks. This was said to be where they could lie down, smoke their opium and not be disturbed. I can't remember that they caused any trouble, and I don't recall the police carrying out a raid there. However, the police on duty in that area always went in twos.

I remember quite well that there were areas where no policeman would show his face without backup. Otherwise, the only way they could get help was to blow their whistle and hope another constable would come to their aid.

~

People did what they thought best for themselves and their family, but this wasn't always best for other people. Some parents taught their children to steal anything that came to hand.

Mrs Gough was one of these. She stitched a large pocket inside her loose-fitting coat, solely to contain the things she thought she needed, but couldn't pay for. She used to tell me about her exploits and curl up with laughter when she thought she had "pulled a fast one" over somebody she didn't like, or thought had too much money. I had to smile at her enjoyment. Her face used to light up like a beacon and I understood how she felt. She knew I would never breathe a word of what she told me, but it was her sheer warmth and innocence which I loved. I always thought it was a privilege to work amongst these wonderful people.

What courage, what resilience! These qualities survive today, but tend to be buried under layers of conformity and only surface in extreme circumstances.

~

One day, as I finished my visits, I got on my bicycle ready to head back along Commercial Road, through Aldgate and the Bank to Victoria, where I could have a cup of tea in peace and write up any notes I hadn't had time for. There was a pet shop fairly near to the Docks and, as I peddled my way past, I happened to see a monkey in the window. Sailors often took animals from the countries they docked in, and on their return to England, they either no longer wanted them or sold them to make money. Snakes and lizards were always popular and there weren't the restrictions which are in place now. The monkey in the window looked pretty aggressive, but had quick movements as if she was interested in everything around her. Against my better judgement, I fell in love. Nobody has ever explained, to my satisfaction, the reason we attach our love to animals, but this felt like pure chemistry. I could see her dear little face in my mind's eye; two quick, darting brown eyes taking everything in. It didn't seem right that a monkey should be in the middle of a city area when the rightful place would be in the wilds of a jungle somewhere.

Once back at the flat in Victoria, I rushed in with my news. "Guess what I've fallen in love with?" I told my husband, who had liberal approach to life. "I know it isn't possible, but I would love to get her out of that awful shop."

"What shop?" he asked. I told him about it, but at the same time realised how difficult it would be to keep a monkey. I thought no more about it.

Getting back home always meant carrying my bike down some stairs to the shed. Going back up to the front door, one day, I heard some loud noises coming from the kitchen. My husband wasn't due back, so I thought I had some unwanted company, like a wino breaking in to get some money for their favourite occupation.

Lo and behold, when I opened the door, there was my monkey chained to the leg of a kitchen chair. He was as wild as a frustrated bull and I rushed to the corner shop, which sold just about everything, to buy some asbestos gloves. At least then I could get hold of her without being bitten. For some reason I named her Bessie, and she became my dearest friend.

She listened to me talking about my days, to the radio about the day's happenings and the problems the government was having trying to get rid of the slums.

I have to say Bessie was quite a handful, and she was a mischievous little thing. She would sit on top of the front door and jump on my head when I entered. She ended up jumping into my arms if she was afraid and it was that that marked our friendship. She was an Indian Rhesus monkey who used to store Maltesers in her cheeks, which puffed them out and made her look funny.

There came a point when, in the enormous cage we had built for her, she would spend half the night "ooing" which I took to be a mating call. It didn't seem fair for her to be alone.

I found out that there was an Indian Rhesus monkey enclosure in Regent's Park Zoo, so I phoned them. The official I spoke to said, "If you can get her here, we'll check her over and put her in quarantine for a short time, then she can go into our enclosure with the other monkeys." I borrowed a wire carrying box for her and took her by underground to Regent's Park Station. It was amusing because there was standing room only on the train, and as I was next to a woman who had lace-up shoes, I saw a brown arm coming through the wire fiddling with the laces. I didn't say anything as the woman might have had hysterics.

A fortnight later I went to see Bessie and took a box of her favourite Maltesers with me. She didn't recognise me and although I felt sad, I was glad that she had the chance to be with her own kind.

After gaining my diploma I became a Queen's
Nurse and life was never dull, but it wasn't always
easy. There were so many patients, in the
community, who needed attention and the conditions some
people lived in were often truly miserable.

One family I visited, the Ritters, had three children, two
of whom were classed, in the language of that time, as
mentally subnormal. The whole family was in poor health.
The youngest child, a little boy who usually looked pale and
sickly, always had a runny nose which never cleared up.

All three children slept in the same room in the same bed.
If one of them had an infection it didn't take long for the
others to catch it.

We had been made aware of the family by a neighbour,
who took pity on them and went to see the local vicar.

It was the early days of the National Health Service and
some people, like this family, didn't understand that medical
and nursing care were free. Despite their constant ill health
they didn't call a doctor for fear they would have to pay.

The vicar contacted us. He was a pleasant young man,
young enough to be shocked at some of the conditions he

saw around him. He was well aware of the reputation of the East End as being full of human depravities, under-age pregnancies, prostitution, illegal abortions, binge-drinking and wife-beating, all in TB-infested slums. Most babies were born at home amongst bed-bugs, maggots, mice and rats.

Whilst all this was true of the East End at that time, the people there struggled valiantly to survive these conditions. There were no-role models for them to copy, no TV. Few people read the papers other than those that involved sport and sex. Children went to school—or didn't. I knew many teachers who breathed a sigh of relief when certain pupils didn't turn up for their lessons.

Like many families, the Ritters only learnt from what was going on around them. They thought it natural for girls and boys to sleep together, especially where space was limited. A lot more support would be available to the Ritters if they had been around now.

In another house I visited Mabel, a large woman with muscles which intimidated many people. I was seeing her about a kidney infection. During my visit the school attendance officer arrived to ask Mabel why her son hadn't attended school for nearly a whole term. She rushed upstairs, retrieved the chamber pot from under the bed, opened the window and tipped the contents on top of his hat, dampening not only the hat and his badge of office, but also his enthusiasm to question her further. She shouted at him, "If you wants my Tommy to come to school you can bleedin' well get 'im some shoes".

A chamber pot was often used in those days by those whose toilets were in the garden or yard, and most were. It wasn't particularly pleasant to have to go outside in the middle of the night, so a pot was a big help especially for those with children.

Some of the children in the East End were very street-wise. They were also light-fingered and often used to study people to find out if there was any chance of stealing something without being caught. Sometimes the children worked together or even with an adult. One would cause a distraction while the other did the stealing. Petticoat Lane market was a typical hunting ground for such thieves. I remember one man threatened to tip over the stall a trader was running. The huge man began throwing things about, whilst a colleague helped himself to some socks from the stall.

~

I'll never know who first called me "The Angel of Aldgate", or why the name caught on. On one occasion it led to a unique incident.

"Let's give 'er an 'alo, " a scruffy-looking urchin shouted to his colleagues, who were playing with old bicycle tyres taken from the local dump .

A shout of glee arose from the group, and as I was pedalling past the infamous Peabody buildings in Aldgate. I was showered with four dirty tyres, as the lads tried unsuccessfully to get one over my head.

With a sigh, I got off my old bicycle and approached the lads, who were beginning to make their escape. I said, "Now then, you rotten lot, isn't it about time you did something useful?"

The boys sniggered and one of them, a small lad wearing a dirty and torn T-shirt, long past its prime, looked up defiantly. "My Dad said 'e's got a chicken you can 'ave. It fell awf the back of a lorry an 'e dun wan' it". He was a lovely lad with a saucy grin that made my heart melt, but at the same time he was a little terror who really enjoyed trying to get me to run after him. My guess was that he and his pals were in cahoots for me to drop my bicycle on the road to run after one of them so that another of them could pinch it and have a ride.

I knew the boy's father, having looked after his wife six months ago. In a drunken argument he had split her lip badly, for which he was deeply repentant, but she never forgave him. She later confided to me that she always put half a cascara tablet (a laxative) in his mug of tea in revenge. It was a small act of retaliation on her part, but it didn't seem to have any effect on him and he certainly didn't seem aware of her little rebellion.

He was a big man with muscles like a rugby player. Though generally friendly, he would purloin anything he could lay hands on. His philosophy was that one should never miss a good opportunity. He appeared to float on the surface of life's quirks, never thinking of such things as cause and effect, or consequences. The idea of honesty seemed entirely alien to him. I remember him saying in his matter-of-fact way, "Well, nurse, if I dun' take it some'un' else will".

Pushing the dirty bicycle tyres away with my foot, I held on to my bike so none of the boys would run off with it.

"Get off with you, you ragbag", I tousled the boy's hair, which felt like a tangle of straw. I was quite fond of these lads. They were always up to mischief, but learning to cope in their world.

The odd cuff round the head was still allowed in those days, but the lads didn't seem to care too much. I often thought they felt rather superior if they had been chastised for something. It gave them some kind of status among their friends.

These boys had a lot to learn just to survive in that area, and I knew it was more important that they learn about real life rather than Pythagoras or the dissolution of the monasteries.

Matt smiled mischievously and raced away with his pals, their dirty old tyres hanging round their necks. I had to grin. These lads were the adults of tomorrow and nobody knew what might be in store for them, but they were preparing themselves.

Certainly they lived in a time of great change. The devastation of WW2 surrounded us in London. There were numerous bomb sites, collecting places for rubbish, pigeons and methylated spirits drinkers. The meths drinkers were hardly sober at any time of the day or night. It was life in the raw, and I felt very proud of these lads who used their guile, skills and cunning to make some kind of a meaningful life for themselves.

I took a deep breath and made my way up the concrete steps to the third floor and door number nineteen. It would have benefited from a coat of paint, but that was the last thing anybody would have done in a building as bleak as this.

I shouted at a stray dog urinating on the walkway. Dogs were always a nuisance as they were often just turned out and left to fend for themselves. It was never easy for the tenants to take a dog for a walk. The owner had to descend several flights of stairs, which smelled foul, and were often covered in rubbish. It was no surprise that Battersea Dogs Home was always bursting at the seams with unwanted dogs. They might look cute when puppies, but they all grow up. At that time puppies were sold in markets, and there was never a shortage.

In flats like these, the lifts, if any, often didn't work. Among other reasons, lads would place a milk bottle between the doors to stop the lift going up or down. This was often done so the young man in question could have a private smooch with his girlfriend.

The whole place was dull and bleak. Smog and coal-smoke had stained the walls; everything was dark and depressing. All the doors to the flats were brown. One or two householders had an aspidistra plant in the window, but they hardly provided the colours needed to brighten the place up. The Peabody Estate was a typical example of the worst Victorian efforts to house too many people in too small an area.

Oddly, this didn't seem to affect the tenants. The families who lived there had a camaraderie you don't see so much of these days. Though grinding poverty was rife, family life was less rushed and people helped each other more.

Women had to share kitchens, and this often led to heated arguments, but also to cooperation.

The women, in buildings like these, seemed to age very quickly as the harsh environment took its toll. It wasn't unusual to see women with scruffy hair in curlers and wearing shabby clothes either too tight or too loose. Nail varnish and make-up were seen very rarely. Washing clothes was a matter of rubbing them on washboards. Sometimes mothers' hands bled with the pressure they had to use when doing laundry and bending over a bath of hot water was crippling for their backs.

Getting to number nineteen to check the progress of a

baby, I saw the neighbour's front door was slightly open. I was fond of the old man, Mr Bernstein, who lived there, and he was the next patient I was going to see. He had had a rotten time in the blitz and lost his wife and daughter when a V2 exploded near their home. He was injured in the blast and still had a limp.

Because he couldn't move very quickly, he left his door ajar so that I could go in without having to wait. That day the door opened only slightly, refusing to budge far enough for me to enter. I pushed and tried to get my arm around the door in an effort to move the blockage. It took some time for me to manage to get hold of what appeared to be a shoe.

Unfortunately my patient was the obstacle. It was obvious from the smell that he had died some time ago. I wondered why nobody had informed the office that he hadn't been seen for a while.

At that moment Matt, having given his tyre a last toss towards a stray dog, came bouncing along the corridor and I asked him to fetch his father. There were no working phones in that building, and I needed help. Matt's father arrived and seemed relieved that brawn rather than brain was required. His strong, heavily-tattooed arms managed to ease Mr Bernstein, inch by inch, away from the door until I could squeeze through and get inside. Matt darted in after me. He stopped with a gasp and, looking up at me in wonderment, said, "E's dead as a dodo ain't 'e?"

I couldn't find a pulse, or detect any breathing, and said to Matt, "I think Mr Bernstein is dead".

"Cor, I ain't seen no stiff afore, but I did see that cat what got run over. 'E looked flat as a pancake."

A note was sent to the doctor and Matt's father helped move Mr Berstein clear so that I could open the door wider.

By the time the nurse and the doctor had finished, it was beginning to get dark. I had had enough for one day, and went down the steps, wearily thinking about the long cycle home, all the way through Aldgate and Westminster and the never-ending traffic.

To my horror, sitting in a cardboard box on the pavement and beside my bicycle, was the promised chicken, very big, and very much alive. I had to see the funny side of it as I had expected the chicken to be dead and my patient alive.

A misty drizzle started to fall and I looked at my chicken and wondered how to transport it back to my house by bicycle. Another local resident, Old Tubby Isaacs, came to my rescue, his broad grin widening as he saw my dilemma.

Tubby was a costermonger that had called me over to his stall one freezing winter day. My feet were so cold and he must have guessed it from my expression as I cycled past. He cut brown paper to fit my shoes and I'll never forget the warmth and relief I felt.

But this day he looked down at the chicken, and said, "Better not leave it 'ere nurse". His huge shoulders heaved as he huffed and puffed due to his asthma. "Let's 'ave a look then". With that, he carefully shifted the unresisting chicken to one side of the box and managed to squeeze my black bag next to it. Then he fastened everything onto the back of my bicycle with cord.

The chicken remained docile and seemingly uncaring as it looked over the edge of the box. There it stayed as I wove in and out of the traffic, the strong cord preventing the box and its contents from falling off the rack.

By the time I got home the chicken had changed its status from that of potential meal to that of spoilt pet named Matilda.

Matilda was made comfortable in the garden shed. Having worked in the operating theatre at UCH, I could never eat anything I had seen blink. Matilda only ever laid one egg, and I couldn't bring myself to cook even that.

One morning it was obvious my little pet was ill. She made strange coughing noises, and ignored the brandy in water I offered, a common cough relief. When I asked the veterinary surgeon for some suitable cough mixture he thought I was making fun of him.

Matilda died behind the shed door, and like Mr Bernstein, she blocked the entrance and made it difficult to get to her.

After a long wet spell, the sun made a welcome appearance and shone over East India Docks. There were a number of boats in to be loaded or unloaded, so many of the men were temporarily employed, heaving sacks and transporting boxes on their shoulders from one place to another, making the most of the cranes which hoisted the large goods from the holds, transferring them to lorries.

Having made good headway with my visits that day, I couldn't resist going over to a crowd of people forming near Poplar Hospital. I could see two police helmets in the crowd, towering above everyone like obelisks. There was an air of excitement and I squeezed between the shopping baskets and waving arms, until I was able see two women rolling on the ground having a no-holds-barred fight. Handfuls of hair and bits of torn clothing flew as the women rolled over and over, punching, biting and screaming at one another. The police didn't interfere, although it was mayhem. They knew only too well that any intervention on their part would lead to the aggression being turned on them, creating further problems. There was an unspoken rule that they didn't get involved unless serious harm was being caused.

It didn't take long for the the two women to collapse exhausted. One of them, dishevelled and with a swollen eye, managed to get to her feet, looked down at her adversary and offered to help her up. As soon as both women were upright, they put their arms around one another and burst into tears. The audience loved it and cheered. The policemen grinned like Cheshire cats and started to move people away. Everyone had had a good morning's entertainment.

I had a new patient on my list that day. Going to a new patient, one never knew what one was going to find. I made my way past Blackwall Tunnel and along Frank Street. These little terraced houses had decades of history in their bricks. This was another dingy area with few of nature's gifts to soften the heart and calm the soul.

One of the things I had learnt was that one should never be fooled by external appearances. The house looked fairly presentable from the outside. There was only about one metre of frontage, which had been thickly concreted to foil any attempts by weeds to push their way through. I wasn't overly surprised to find the front door ajar and, as I knocked, a voice from one of the bedrooms called me to go up. There were no carpets on the dirty floorboards and the stairs were littered with rubbish, which exuded a smell somewhat like sulphur. When I got to the bedroom I found a man in his forties surrounded by beer bottles, all empty. They were on the floor, the dirty bed, and under it.

This patient was prescribed daily intramuscular injections of procaine penicillin. It wasn't a particularly easy medicine to give, as it was a very thick solution. The secret was to draw it into the syringe using a large needle, then to swap the needle to a less painful one for injection. As I was preparing the sterile needles the man jumped out of bed naked and came at me, his filthy hands waving around like windmills.

I turned quickly and pushed him back towards the bed, "Now then, Mr Bearman, if you don't have this injection right now you are going to be very ill. Lie face down." Fortunately the man did as he was told, but I wasn't too sure how long his cooperation would last, so I decided to dampen his ardour. I didn't change the large needle and with a good swing inserted it into his backside. The procaine penicillin flowed in beautifully and I left him to his discomfort, saying, "That's right, give it a good rub Mr Bearman". With that I quickly disappeared, manoeuvring past the rubbish on the stairs and out into the road. By the time my patient had recovered his sang-froid I was well on my way to the next patient, Mrs Cohen.

She was a dear old lady, who lay in bed in a room dominated and made gloomy and claustrophobic by a huge aspidistra plant. When I had visited her for the first time, two days before, she had been in a fairly poor state.

I had pulled back the dirty, damp bedclothes and saw Mrs Cohen's oedema was so bad that her swollen legs were literally oozing fluid. This had encouraged flies to lay eggs and create a colony of maggots. I changed the bedclothes, dealt with the oedema, and asked Mrs Cohen where her clean linen was. She pointed to a large mahogany chest and I found clean sheets, and a cotton nightdress with frills around the neck. I also found many rolls of pound notes in the back of the drawer. This was not unusual in the East End as few people trusted banks. Also, it was possibly money the Inland Revenue knew nothing about.

It took a long time to deal with Mrs Cohen's condition that day, but when I had finished, she looked beautiful. Her legs were treated with dressings and medication, she and her bed were clean, and her once-matted hair was brushed and plaited. She sat up in bed smiling and happy.

Now, two days later, I propped my bicycle against the railings and called as I entered the open door. On going into the room I was faced with an enormous gorilla of man in no happy frame of mind. "What do you mean by puttin' that nightdress on me mother. I was savin' that to lay 'er awt in".

I looked at the man and said, "I really don't think you have to worry too much about that for a long time, Mr. Cohen." I looked at his mother and winked. Mrs Cohen smiled with delight. No words were necessary.

~

One day, looking down my growing list of patients, I noticed that Dr Chazen had added yet another patient for me to visit and I knew it would to be a long day.

Mary, who ran the office, was apologetic. "He didn't think you'd mind this one, Jean, as it isn't too far off Mare Street". I liked Dr Chazen; we often managed to have discussions about problem patients, and he was always happy to give me more.

It is really strange how buildings can project atmosphere, and the area this client lived in gave me a feeling of unease. The alleyways were dark, and the large warehouses, used for storage of imported goods, stretched high between narrow roads and blocked much of the daylight. I was always pleased to move on to patients in other areas.

Taking my list from Mary, I looked at the name of my new patient, Mrs Margaret Brooks. Once I had finished my other visits, I made my way to Ryan's Road. It was a miserable day and the sun had had great difficulty finding its way through the mist. The fumes of buses and lorries shrouded the gateway to the docks and drifted towards Plaistow and Barking.

It was with a sigh of relief that I rang the bell of the grubby little two-up-two-down terraced house. I rang the bell three times, before I heard panting and puffing as the door slowly opened. "Hello, Mrs Brooks, Dr Chazen has asked me to syringe your eye for you." I smiled at the woman but there was no response apart from a nod. She didn't speak and, as she went back into the house, I noticed she used her hands to feel her way along the wall and manoeuvre herself into the kitchen at the end of the passageway.

I followed her and, as she turned round, realised she had not one, but two artificial eyes. Dr Chazen hadn't warned me that two sockets needed attention. I opened my bag and got out the kidney dish, syringe and sterile, half-strength saline. "Have you a towel I can put over your shoulders, Mrs Brook, just to stop your jumper getting wet?" She gave me a small piece of towelling and I placed a piece of Jaconet, a sterile dressing, on top of it.

I eased down the left lower lid and extricated the left eye. Then I did the same with the right and placed both of them in a small dish, making sure they were covered with sterile water. After syringing the sockets I checked that there was no infection and proceeded to replace the eyes. The situation was a useful learning curve as I had naively removed both eyes before syringing the sockets. It is amazing how many permutations you can have with one eye, let alone two. There is the right and the left, and the top and the bottom. To complicate things further, the pupils looked focussed, so they didn't appear too blank. It took me ages to get them in the correct positions, and she seemed to be either squinting or cross-eyed when I got it wrong.

Finally, Mrs Brooks was happy that her eyes were in the position which felt right for her. She wanted me to call her "Margaret" and joined my list of regular patients.

I have to admit that I became fairly expert at removing eyes and replacing them, but only one at a time. I had to smile, remembering how I'd criticised student nurses for mixing up people's dentures.

I have always thought how dreadful it must be to have no sight. Certainly Margaret had no idea that the water from her cold tap was full of rust and didn't clear until about a gallon had run through. What it did to her digestion and food was something to brush aside and not think about, although I did mention it to Dr Chazen. My only hope was that the feverish rebuilding of bomb-damaged areas in London would produce some kind of accommodation for her quickly, but this took two years.

~

Fred and Mavis Sykes were two of my patients. Their circumstances and relationship were such that life was going to be pretty rough for both of them. They lived in a damp and cramped rented property. This needn't have been the case as Fred was a member of the Watermen, Lightermen, Tugmen and Bargemen's Union and such men had reasonably paid jobs working on the Thames in boats of various kinds, and sometimes helping the river police solve crimes.

Fred suffered migraine attacks which were often triggered by the kind of work he had to do and also by Mavis who, to put it mildly, was referred to as a shrew by Fred's colleagues.

Her assertiveness would have made her an excellent "Women's Rights" campaigner, another Emmeline Pankhurst, but she did sometimes create conflict where there was no need, and if she had just thought about the situation a little and not been so trigger-happy, the problem her husband had might have been less severe.

Her main problem was that she felt Fred earned enough money to rent them a much better place and she bitterly resented living in their mean housing. She believed Fred wasted a lot of money in the local pub, drinking. He also smoked Woodbines until, according to her, "They came out of 'is ears".

Fred was beefy, with muscles which hurt you just to look at them. He had dark curly hair which used to curl even more when he perspired with effort, or rage. His face was expressive and easy to read. I often felt that Mavis would have been wiser to read the signs and make things easier for herself.

I wondered at one time if Mavis and Fred would end up killing one another, Mavis lacking both intelligence and sensitivity, and Fred with his enormous calloused hands which could have ended anybody's life with just a squeeze or a thump.

Sometimes Mavis had the sense to defuse an argument by hiding in the church. There had been one or two occasions when someone had run down to the police station to get a policeman involved, but again in those days they wouldn't interfere with family squabbles between husband and wife. I came across many "battered wives" and it wasn't easy to deal with situations in which one couldn't see or assess the whole picture.

Fred and Mavis created a very complicated picture.

The complexity increased with the birth of their son Jack. He had been a forceps delivery and suffered from cerebral irritation which caused him to scream with pain. Mavis used to walk the floor with him day and night and became very tired and run down. To top it all Jack was fed National Dried Milk which was the most common and cheapest available, but wasn't always right for sensitive stomachs.

Fred's devastating migraines caused not only a physically debilitation, but had a social impact. Migraines were thought to be a female problem in those days and consequently they conflicted with his macho image.

In those days things like relaxation, yoga, acupuncture, tai chi, and even osteopathy were either not known about or thought to be somewhat weird. Consequently he was a man who had to sort himself out and couldn't. This caused feelings of failure on top of everything else. Sometimes, for pain relief, he would bang his head against a wall. This often triggered his rages, which could be extreme when not handled properly. Mavis was far too insensitive to be of any help.

They both could have done with psychotherapy, but nobody trusted anything like that.

After a gruelling night, Fred, unable to bear the high-pitched screams any longer, picked Jack up out of his cot and flung him across the room, where he hit the wall and lay still and silent where he fell.

An ambulance was called and Jack, along with his shocked parents, were taken to Poplar Hospital casualty department.

Fortunately it was found that little Jack was only suffering from mild concussion and the doctors told his parents it was necessary to keep him in for observation. One of his legs had received a bang as he landed against the wall, but apart from that he seemed to have survived, much to Fred's relief.

The police had not been involved and the incident wasn't taken any further other than the Almoner, along with one of the Casualty doctors having a quiet word with both parents about Jack's care.

Doctor Chazen asked me to go every day to check on the family.

It was understood at the time that child-battering occurred more often when high frequency crying or screaming was involved. This high frequency, which arises due to the vocal chords of the baby being tightened, stressed those exposed to it.

This was explained Fred and Mavis who were advised to put Jack in his pram and take him out to relieve the tension in the house and be settled by the motion of the pram.

Once little Jack returned home, I showed Mavis how to pre-digest his feeds with a product called Benger's. This contained wheat-flour and an extract of pancreatic juice, which partially digested the proteins present in milk and made it easier for young babies to tolerate. It was also helpful to raise Jack's head in his cot to help relieve any pressure. An anti-inflammatory gel helped with his teething, and Jack gradually became a calmer baby, much to the relief of his parents.

Once Doctor Chazen and I were happy with the situation I reduced my visits and was pleased to learn that Mavis had got her way and she, Fred and Jack had acquired better accommodation which I felt would make life easier for all three of them.

~

One of my patients, Olive, was as thin as a rake, but when roused, could throw as good a punch as any man. Her clothes hung on her like limp washing, but her children were her life. Whilst she welcomed new a new child into her life, she had great difficulty providing enough for them to eat, and priority was given to her husband who had to have the energy to do his job when he was chosen at the docks to load freight.

She had suffered a uterine prolapse which didn't improve and it gave her a great deal of discomfort. I don't know how she managed to keep as cheerful as she did. She needed surgery, but refused to go into hospital. The Salvation Army were supportive of her and gave her clothes for the children if they needed things like warm jumpers and scarves. Sometimes they would present her with some meat and vegetables to help feed the family.

I grew to admire Olive. She was a lovely woman, a strong, caring person who epitomised the people who survived uncomplaining and were willing to help other people in that tough world.

~

It was the beginning of one November and, along with the worsening weather, there came the problems of colds and coughs. Added to these were the greater threats of pneumonia, bronchitis and tuberculosis.

It was never too pleasant cycling in the damp and cold atmosphere. When the roads were wet, whenever a car, bus or lorry overtook me, water splashed up my leg. I learned that it was a good idea to take a small towel with me so I could dry off every so often. My trips backwards and forwards to my patients were often hard and took their toll. The fumes from the buses and cars hung like curtains and sometimes made breathing difficult even for me. They affected those with respiratory diseases far more.

Fairly regularly I would visit a patient only to find the whole family suffering from an extreme bout of viral influenza. The children would be coughing and sneezing, with very little opportunity to use handkerchiefs. Very often the children shared a bed and infection ran riot among them. Needless to say it was hit and miss as to whether or not I would be infected by whatever they had, but I was always careful to do whatever I could to avoid illness.

As Christmas reared its head, I enjoyed the rising excitement of the children. In those days they were thrilled to get an orange and some sweets in the bottom of a stocking. It was so different to the expectations of children now, where there is so much more available for them. I often wonder if, in those days where we valued everything much more, people were happier.

I felt very guilty about the gifts my patients showered on me, and I worried that they felt it a duty. I spoke to Dr Chazen about it and he laughed out loud. "Put yourself in their place. The East Enders, the Cockneys, are made of stoic stuff. They survived the war and are self-motivated. It makes them feel good to give you something back for all that you do for them."

At that time I didn't have many people who needed daily

injections or treatment, so I managed to take some time off on Christmas Day and took the chance to catch up on some sleep.

I had several patients with ulcers of one kind or another. A new dressing was being introduced for these. It was sterile gauze and Vaseline dressing. It came in a flat tin with a layer of sterile grease-proof paper between each sheet. I had to make certain that if one layer was removed I didn't contaminate the others. It really did help tremendously and ulcers, which would have continued to suppurate and cause much pain, began to heal. Mrs Coster had shouted, "I fought me bleedin leg would 'ave to be cut awf. Now look nurse, when we gets warm wevver, I can leave me stockins awf. Me 'usband's goin' to 'ave a shock. Somethin' to tell 'em at the pub". Her face lit up and she gave me such a wonderful brown, toothy grin, the gaps revealing the results of her arguments with her stevedore husband, a giant of a man who thought nothing of employing his extremely strong muscles on her.

~

One day I was asked to go to a convent in Aldgate and give a nun a blanket bath. To be honest I was a bit dismayed as I felt it was an intrusion on my time when I had so many sick people to visit and treat. It was the only time in my nursing career I have refused to help. I felt that the woman was surrounded by other women who could quite easily have seen to her. More important to me was to see to those who really needed medical care. I was overloaded with work. I felt my stance on this was justified. I didn't like being used, and was pleased when the Mother Superior found another solution.

Looking back, I realise my anger to this request arose from the pressure of the job, which was too much sometimes. It isn't easy to deal with people who lived in such desperate circumstances, and I often felt I could have done with some emotional support. In reality it was a question of sweeping things under the proverbial carpet and working on regardless.

~

The London Smog was thought to have killed over 12,000 people in December 1952. That was a lot more than died during an average smog.

It was caused by an unusually cold spell and Londoners used more and more coal on their fires to try to keep warm. All the smoke, along with the factory emissions, was prevented from escaping into the atmosphere and the fog and smoke combined into a thick layer of smog.

Each day of the smog, thousands upon thousands of tons of pollutants, including carbon dioxide, hydrochloric acid, fluorine compounds, and sulphur dioxide, which converted to sulphuric acid, were added to the increasingly poisonous air.

My patients were used to the well-known pea-soup fogs, but this one was different and far more lethal to the elderly, those who had a poor immune system, and especially those with lung conditions such as pulmonary TB.

Visibility was down to one foot. Few people dared venture out in case they lost their way, as eyes were of little use. It was hard to see your hand in front of your face.

The silence was unnerving. There were no buses, trams,

trains, ambulances, and few pedestrians. The silent city gave one an eerie feeling that something awful was going to happen.

As I pushed my bike along, no longer able to see where I was going, I sometimes heard footsteps, but it was impossible to make out where they were coming from, or going, and I tried to peer into the blackness to find my way home.

I knew my patients would have trouble with their breathing. There isn't much oxygen in the black haze of smog, so I tried to see as many of my more vulnerable patients as I could. It was a nightmare and the dark of night-time made the situation far worse.

A desperate patient asked his wife to go next door to the "Salt-Beef Café" which was run by a chap called Amos. He had a phone and my patient's wife asked him to phone the BBC London programme to try to contact Nurse Sonntag, who was known locally as The Angel of Aldgate. They thought I may hear the call on the radio, and that I might be able to get to them.

Doctors, fire-fighters, police and the boats on the Thames with their mournful hooting were as good as helpless. People who had gone to work often couldn't leave as there was no transport and it was easy to get lost, even in familiar streets.

One of the most amazing things that happened to me at this time occurred near to the Houses of Parliament where I was struggling to decide which way to try getting back to Victoria. The silence was absolute and I did feel a bit anxious. Suddenly I heard a voice calling my name out of the blackness. I couldn't believe it. After a moment, I realised the voice was that of my husband, Erich, who was trying to find me. He appeared just like a miracle and it was such a comfort to have his support in trying to get home.

By the time we did get back, we were both covered in pollution and, when I took off my cap, there was a very marked line across my forehead, white where my cap protected my upper forehead and almost black where my face was exposed.

I didn't hear the broadcast until the following day and, even then, couldn't get to my patient until two days later.

We were all pushed to our limits, but as soon as I could, I went to see Amos to thank him, and also my patient's wife who had braved the few steps to his shop. Amos, like the well-rounded generous man he was, insisted I left with the biggest salt-beef sandwich I had ever seen. It had boosted him to think he had been of use.

The undertakers were busy the following week with a glut of people to bury, but the one thing positive about it all was that because of the horror, the government came up with better regulations for coal burning, and the idea of smokeless fuel was born.

~

After several years of happiness working with the East Londoners it was the discovery that my husband had been taken to the Middlesex Hospital with a suspected heart attack that made me realise I needed to be more available for him. The authorities had been unable to contact me as I was working and most people didn't have phones. So after much thought and discussion I resigned from the East London section of the Queen's Institute of District Nursing and was offered the post of Ward Sister in the Men's Surgical ward at Poplar Hospital.

My last day as a community nurse was exceedingly sad and arms were thrown round me by many of my patients.

It had been the building of trusting relationships with them which was so wonderful. It had also been a time of exciting development within the NHS. The families, which had had to cope without a doctor because they were too poor, now had access to health care.

For some people it was a revolution - for instance, mothers receiving the vitamins and minerals they needed during pregnancy.

What stands out from my whole experience as a Queen's Nurse is the spirit of the East End population. The support they gave each other during this time of poverty and deprivation. I learned to appreciate how much just a little help and support means to people who are struggling. The world can be a difficult place for anybody and I was inspired to help people wherever and whenever I could.

~

It doesn't matter where one lives, and it doesn't matter how much money one has in the bank or what position one has in any society, there are certain human needs essential to us all.

To be cared for, respected and to have the attention you need, are fundamental to a patient's well-being and recovery.

Nurses care very much about the well-being and happiness of those we treat. A hand placed gently on someone's head or arm conveys messages which no medicine or instrument can. Body-language and facial expression are powerful tools when helping people.

Though nurses have taken on many of the jobs done in the past by doctors, this should never be at the expense of basic nursing care – the skill of providing comfort, dignity and the feeling of being cared for.

These are as vital in a patient's treatment as medicine and surgery. The research on placebos has gone a long way to reinforce this.

It was the Dalai Lama who, when asked what is the meaning of life, said, "Happiness. It is a question all human beings must try to answer. Money? big house? accomplishment? or passion and a big heart?" He gave emphasis to the last two and then fell silent, with a knowing smile on his face.

Acknowledgements

I would like to thank Gary Bonn for his ongoing support and efficiency in helping me to complete this short story about my work in the East End of London and the NHS in the 1950s. The world has changed a great deal but human needs remain the same. I sincerely hope that we don't get too caught up in the technology which denies the importance of acceptance, understanding and care which helps to make a society one can be proud of.

I would also like to thank all those wonderful people who taught me so much about life and the way in which the human condition can overcome most of the difficulties one encounters.

About The Author

Jean Audrey Wilson was born in London in 1930 when society was recovering from the Great Depression. She lived through the horrors of the Blitz in which London, particularly the East End docks where she lived, was devastated by thousands of bombs dropped by the Luftwaffe.

The stoicism and spirit of the Cockneys ignited her deep interest in people and all through her life she has endeavoured to unlock the mysteries of human behaviour.

After years of nursing she trained as a teacher, later taking a degree in Educational Psychology, followed by the University of London Diploma in the Education of Handicapped Children. She was an examiner for various examination boards and was involved in Sir Keith Joseph's efforts to break the "Cycle of Deprivation".

Jean, who was accepted by the British Psychological Society for testing, also undertook the testing of prisoners released from prison in order to channel them into most suitable work.

New findings and research into brain chemistry are beginning to increase our ability to help people, but they also expose many gaps in our knowledge.

Jean hopes she has enough years left to make some inroads into those gaps, in order to contribution to their solution.

Made in the USA
Charleston, SC
16 September 2014